SEE YOURSELF
THROUGH GOD'S EYES

SEE YOURSELF THROUGH GOD'S EYES

52 Meditations to Grow in Self-Esteem

By Marie Paul Curley, FSP

Pauline

BOOKS & MEDIA

Boston

Cover design by Rosana Usselmann

Cover photo: Klaus Larsen Photography / istockphoto.com

"P" and PAULINE are registered trademarks of the Daughters of St. Paul.

Copyright © 2009, Daughters of St. Paul

Published by Pauline Books & Media, 50 Saint Pauls Avenue, Boston, MA 02130-3491

Printed in the U.S.A.

www.pauline.org

Pauline Books & Media is the publishing house of the Daughters of St. Paul, an international congregation of women religious serving the Church with the communications media.

5 6 7 8 9 10   22 21 20 19 18

———◂◦▸———

To the Sisters of my community,
the Daughters of St. Paul—
for the ways you share
the love of Christ with me
and with the world.

———◂◦▸———

Contents

Introduction *1*

PART 1

THE GOD WHO LOVES ME

1. God loves me for who I am *9*

2. God is faithful *11*

3. God loves me unconditionally in my weakness *14*

4. God shows his love for me every day *17*

5. God lovingly provides for all my needs *19*

6. In God's eyes, I am worthy *22*

7. I trust in the ways God works in my life *25*

8. God wants my deepest happiness *27*

9. God wants to speak heart to heart with me *30*

10. God lovingly provides for me in every circumstance *32*

11. No worry or fear can separate me from God's love *35*

12. God lovingly chose to create me *37*

13. God invites me to accept myself as I am *40*

14. God calls me to live in love *42*

15. God rejoices when I seek forgiveness 45

16. I remember how blessed I am 48

17. God's love is my security 50

18. God's love is a never-ending stream flowing
    through my life 53

PART 2

SHAPING MY IDENTITY IN CHRIST

19. My hopes and disappointments open my heart
    to the blessings of God 59

20. God lovingly restores me to life 61

21. I appreciate the people God has put in my life 64

22. I entrust my burdens to Jesus 67

23. I let go of needing perfect results,
    entrusting them to God 69

24. I thank God for making me unique 72

25. Silence invites me to remember God's
    loving kindness 75

26. My weaknesses can be entryways for God's grace 78

27. God's mercy is greater than my sinfulness 80

28. God gives me feelings to enrich my life
    and shape my actions 83

29. God invites me to walk through fear into trust 86

30. Loneliness puts me in touch with my need
    to connect 88

31. I can use criticism as an invitation to learn *91*

32. I acknowledge my dependence on God and others *94*

33. From within the pain of loss, I can treasure the gift
     I have received *96*

34. I look for the beauty of God's presence
     in the world *99*

35. I cling to God's steadfastness in times of change *101*

36. I invite Jesus to teach me to be gentle *104*

37. I entrust what is beyond my control to God *107*

PART 3

GOD'S BELOVED IN THE WORLD

38. I live in touch with my own truth wherever I am *113*

39. I accept both my giftedness and weakness,
     secure in God's love *115*

40. In sufferings, I can count on God's special
     closeness to me *118*

41. God cares about my intentions and efforts,
     not whether I succeed *121*

42. I live in the truth of who Jesus calls me to be
     in the world *123*

43. I seek to fulfill my God-given potential *126*

44. I accept responsibility for my choices,
     not those of others *128*

45. Forgiveness empowers and frees me *131*

46. I count on God's faithfulness in my sufferings *134*

47. When doubts overwhelm me, I seek refuge
    in Jesus *137*

48. God wants to give me the joy of following
    my dreams *139*

49. I choose to be guided by the light of God's love *142*

50. God works through both my successes and failures ... *145*

51. I trust that God gives me the grace for the challenges
    I face *147*

52. I accept Jesus' invitation to live in him *150*

Conclusion: A New Beginning *153*

Appendix A: Suggestions for Praying
with Sacred Scripture *155*

Appendix B: Additional Resources *163*

Topical Index *165*

Introduction

Recently, I met a young pastor whom I have come to admire. In just a couple of years, he has revitalized his parish. His parishioners love him, both for his dynamic preaching and, more importantly, for the way he witnesses to God's love for us. Yet, he confided to me, "I am surer that God has called me to be a priest than I am of God's personal love for me."

His honesty saddened and comforted me. I was saddened for what he suffers, but I was comforted because he reminded me that I am not the only one to have devastating doubts harass my joy and peace. All of us at times share in this struggle to believe that God loves us. It becomes particularly urgent or painful when we experience personal tragedy, attempt to cope with loss, or confront our inner darkness and sinfulness. And for some of us, this kind of doubt about our own lovability is not occasional, but a painful way of life.

This little book grew out of my own struggles to accept God's love for me and develop a positive self-esteem. Discovering God's love has taken me on an amazing journey from self-hate to a positive self-acceptance. I wish I'd had a resource like this at the beginning of my journey, something that could have helped me cling to the seemingly impossible reality of God's love for me.

Like many people, I have struggled with low self-esteem for much of my life. For years, I naively thought that others did not have this struggle. I just knew that, ever since I could remember, I felt inadequate to life's challenges, ashamed of revealing anything about myself because others would find out how shallow and unworthy of being loved I really was. The simple challenges of everyday life were enough to cue taunting voices of self-doubt or even self-hate. I was rarely at ease with myself. Trying something new was incredibly anxiety-provoking. By the time I was a teenager, low self-esteem had become a distorted mirror that prevented me from being able to see myself honestly, despite the love of my family and friends, my good grades at school, and the volunteer work I enjoyed.

Although I could not clearly recognize my gifts, I did allow them to lead me to my vocation, and I eventually entered religious life. But in my preparation to become a Daughter of Saint Paul, I continued to doubt that I was lovable. My doubts ran so deep that, despite how important to me my relationship with God was becoming, I still didn't believe God could love me.

I needed to experience being loved unconditionally by Someone who could not be wrong about me, Someone whose judgment was unquestionable and whose fidelity I could cling to. As I continued to deepen my relationship with God, guided by the wisdom and gentleness of my spiritual director, I realized that the only way I could indisputably challenge my relentless self-doubt was to discover who I was in God's eyes.

With help from the classes and personal guidance I received, I gradually came to identify the root of my lack of self-confidence as poor self-esteem. I also became aware of how low self-esteem prevented me from being at peace with myself and caused me to live in a state of high anxiety.

My first big breakthrough was a powerful and intimate prayer experience in which I gazed into the eyes of Jesus and discovered how cherished I was. The Lord's no-conditions-asked, immensely personal love for me was powerfully healing and transforming. Little by little, I found my shame and self-hatred diminishing. I began to experience the world with less fear and more joy.

I also realized that while I could come to the truth about myself within my relationship with God, I needed to accompany my meditation on God's love with some necessary personal inner work. Low self-esteem had warped my perceptions not only of myself, but also of God and others. Small events of daily life could trigger a disproportionate emotional response in me. I realized that I needed help to come to terms with my past. I began counseling to address my psychological needs.

My journey of inner healing needed my faith to give it purpose, meaning, and hope. Focusing on God's love for me gave me the security to continue on the journey, daring to begin to love myself and to hope that the darkness on the journey would not last forever. Counseling opened me up to a deeper and more positive relationship with myself and the Lord.

Today, I still need to work daily to strengthen my conviction that God loves me, but I find myself increasingly open to his love. I'm able to respond to the challenges in my life rather than run away from them, and this reinforces my self-respect and healthy self-esteem. Joy seeps in unexpectedly, filling the corners and pockets of my life in countless ways. God's love for me has become the bedrock of my identity, my spiritual life, and a healthier self-esteem.

One of the biggest helps on this journey of learning to love and value myself as God does was praying with the Word of God. The Scripture passages and meditations included in *See Yourself Through God's Eyes* are some of the lifelines that have helped me to trust in God's love.

I've divided this book into three parts:

The meditations in Part 1, "The God Who Loves Me," focus on how God expresses his love for us through the Scriptures and encourage us to trust in that love.

Part 2, "Shaping My Identity in Christ," helps us to see who we are in the light of God's unconditional love and in the daily events that shape our lives, such as friendships, disappointments, successes, and failures.

The meditations in Part 3, "God's Beloved in the World," highlight the consequences of our being loved unconditionally and encourage us to live this conviction of God's love for us in the world.

The 52 meditations can be used daily, weekly, or from time to time—whenever we need a reminder of God's love for us. Each meditation is broken down into four steps, or moments:

1. A story or example from ordinary life situations that can reveal negative or false patterns of thinking about ourselves or God. Some stories are from my own life; many are stories others have shared with me. I begin with everyday experiences because that's where God is present, even though we often misinterpret our experiences or miss God altogether.

In the stories, I have changed significant details and circumstances to protect others' privacy, but the truth or insight as it was experienced is faithfully preserved.

2. *From God's Heart to Yours:* A passage from the Scriptures in which God speaks heart to heart with us and sheds light on the situation, assumptions, or feelings that the first part raises. Though it's short, this second part is the heart of the meditation because as Christians we know that the inspired Word of God has the power to transform us.

3. *Hidden in the Darkness:* A reflection that allows the Scripture passage to challenge or speak directly to the false assumptions under which we tend to interpret our daily experience. The title and approach to this part are inspired by a passage from Isaiah: "I will go before you and level the mountains.... I will give you the treasures of darkness" (Isa 45:2–3). God delights in using the very issues and situations that challenge us most as opportunities to

help us grow. The darkness where God seems absent is a sacred place where we can discover the hidden treasure of God's loving and faithful presence. We simply need to allow the light of the Scriptures to illumine the darkness.

4. *Through the Day:* A short prayer to reconnect us throughout the day to God's love and fidelity.

For those who would like to delve deeper into praying with the Scriptures, I've provided some additional suggestions in Appendix A, "Suggestions for Praying with Sacred Scripture."

My hope and prayer for you is that this little book will enable you to grow in healthy self-esteem and, above all, to recognize how tremendously God loves and cherishes you. As God's love heals our deepest wounds, we are released from our shame and self-hatred. We no longer need to focus on fear or protecting ourselves. Free and joyful, we radiate the love God has shared with us. As a stone thrown into a pond creates ever-widening ripples, God's unconditional love radiates from us and through us, touching others' lives. May these ripples of God's love continue to widen so they touch, surround, and transform the entire world.

PART 1

THE GOD
WHO LOVES ME

1 God loves me for who I am.

"I wish I had more self-confidence."

My heart is pounding, my palms sweaty, my fingers cold as ice, and I cannot quite take in a full breath of air. I am standing in general assembly on my first day of first grade, waiting with hundreds of kids to be divided into our various classes, and I am terrified.

I'm not just afraid of the usual things, like talking to the teacher, or meeting my new classmates, or the schoolwork. What I am truly terrified of is that I will do something unforgivably horrible or stupid that will definitively prove to the world that I am worthless.

I am sure that everyone remembers being scared and nervous as a child, but I suspect not every child is as haunted as I was by such a strong sense of inadequacy. Some of us struggle more than others with feelings of inadequacy, guilt, and self-doubt throughout our lives. My journal still includes occasional confessions like: "I don't know what I'm doing." "I feel so stupid." "It's all my fault." "I know I'm going to fail."

It took me a long time to realize that my feelings of inadequacy are simply feelings. They can't show me the full truth about myself—who I am in God's eyes. The Scriptures repeatedly remind me of the truth that no matter what I think of myself, God always loves me.

From God's Heart to Yours

"[Y]ou are precious in my sight, and honored, and I love you" (Isa 43:4).

Hidden in the Darkness

This passage from Isaiah reveals the Lord's startling attitude to the Chosen People *and* to each of us: the almighty Creator of heaven and earth doesn't take us for granted but cherishes us and delights in who we are. God sets no conditions for loving us. God doesn't need us to have a good opinion of ourselves in order to love us. Even in the darkness of low self-esteem, God loves us.

Our self-image reflects one, or maybe several, aspects of our identity, as a pencil sketch gives an impression of a mountainside. But God doesn't need a sketch. God walks on the mountainside and sees it from every angle, in all its glorious colors and majesty, from every point in time. God knows us better than we could ever know ourselves. God sees us as we truly are: our inner essence, our entire history, our longings, our gifts, our potential, and our woundedness. And God finds us beautiful. The language used in Isaiah—even in such a short statement—is tenderly extravagant.

The Word of God can powerfully transform us if we let it in, past our inner defenses.

How can we allow God's love into the picture we have of ourselves?

We can start now by taking a moment to simply stay with these words from Isaiah, hearing God speak them to us in the depths of our hearts…

If that is too difficult, we can take a moment to think of someone who is dear to us, perhaps remembering our last conversation, or the ways that person has enriched our life.

Now, we imagine God bringing us to mind in the same way.

We can take joy today that God sees into the very core of who we are, and cherishes us.

Through the Day

Lord, I rejoice in your love for me.

————◄○►————

2 God is faithful.

"I can't trust anybody."

My friend is uncharacteristically late in meeting me for a leisurely cup of tea. Tara is a beautiful and talented young woman who is energetically pursuing her dream to become an artist. When she finally arrives, I see that her fine features are troubled—her face does not reflect her usual serenity. She blurts out, "I've moved out of my mom's house."

Surprised by her sudden decision, I ask, "Why?" Hesitantly, Tara reveals that her mother has been physically abusive toward her for years. Finally, her mother hit her one too many times, and Tara realized it was time to move out.

She looks at me, waiting for my reaction. I take her hand and squeeze it. "I'm so sorry, but I'm glad you moved out so you can start to feel safe."

The opaqueness in her eyes fades and, for a moment, I glimpse her pain and sense of loss. She adds the heart-piercing question, "If everyone else thinks I'm okay, then why doesn't my mother like me?"

Tara's question expresses the need we all have to be loved by our parents. But Tara doesn't deserve the kind of self-doubt buried within that question. She seems to suspect everyone else is wrong; it is her mother who is right.

Being hurt by someone we love is a risk in every relationship, because we are imperfect. But even when someone we trust seems to reject us, God *never* could.

From God's Heart to Yours

"Do not cast me off, do not forsake me, O God of my salvation! / If my father and mother forsake me, the LORD *will take me up" (Ps 27:9–10).*

Hidden in the Darkness

The psalmist recognizes that human love is imperfect, and rarely unconditional. The love of a parent for a child might be the closest human love comes to being divine, but even when it is not flawed, it always has limits. Deep down, we know this as children; we fear to be rejected by those we love. Yet, there is an all-faithful One who deserves all our trust.

It's natural to base our ideas of God's love on the love we received from our parents. But as we mature, we realize that the reverse is true: our triune God's love is the model for all human love. Human love is a small likeness of God's astonishingly faithful and completely unconditional love. God gives himself in love to us in myriad ways: from the gift of our very existence to the beautiful world we live in, from the countless little joys threading through an ordinary day to the unsurpassable gift of God's self-revelation throughout salvation history.

God wants to be united with us so urgently that the Son of God took on and shares our humanity. Jesus' entire life, but especially his passion, death, and resurrection, is a mystery to ponder over and over again, a constant proof that our faithful God could never abandon us.

When we feel the pain of rejection or abuse, or the limitations of another person's love for us, we can remind ourselves that in Jesus, we have proof that God will never reject us, that God always understands us, that God is tenderly faithful and always on our side.

Through the Day

> Jesus, Image of the Father's faithful love, I trust in you.

---

3 God loves me unconditionally in my weakness.

"I shouldn't make mistakes!"

Miriam is a young mother with two little ones: mischievous Peter, who is three, and strong-willed Katherine, who is five. As for many mothers with toddlers, Miriam's greatest struggle is with patience.

One afternoon the house keys disappear. Miriam gently asks Peter if he played with the keys. Sensing trouble, Peter shakes his head. Katherine confides, "I saw Peter playing with them, but I think he forgot." Miriam resigns herself to searching Peter's favorite hiding places, but she can't find them anywhere. After an hour or two of searching, Miriam stops stifling all her sighs and grunts. An hour later, Miriam slams a few drawers and a closet door. Finally, after four interminable hours, she notices that the bottom drawer of a filing cabinet is cracked open, and she rescues the keys from a file folder. Katherine, greatly impressed, brings her mother a lollipop and tells her, "Good job!" At that, Miriam almost bursts into tears.

Miriam has succeeded in not losing her temper. But she feels she failed because her children were able to tell she was upset. How many times we think one mistake outweighs everything else we do. Sometimes, making a mistake can trigger the familiar but devastating conviction that we *are* the mistake. But this is not what the Scriptures tell us.

From God's Heart to Yours

"For the mountains may depart and the hills be removed, / but my steadfast love shall not depart from you.... O afflicted one, storm-tossed, and not comforted" (Isa 54:10–11).

Hidden in the Darkness

In these moving words, God sympathizes with the Chosen People who have, once again, been unfaithful in following God's way. They have messed up—and this is God's surprising response. These words aren't the condemnation of a judge, but the tender sympathy of a Lover for his beloved.

Our image of the infinite God is always limited and inadequate. For example, how do we comprehend the seemingly contradictory statements that God is all-just and all-loving? From our human perspective, these are opposites. But in God, they are united: God's justice is an expression of his love for us, and God's love is reflected in his justice. The point of God's justice is to "make things right" for us, his beloved ones.

God is not, as some of us imagine, like a judge in an Olympic competition. God does not give marks for our performance, scrutinizing our mistakes and replaying them from every angle. Instead, God is always gazing lovingly into our hearts. Because God—the only One who doesn't make mistakes—is our Creator, we could never, ever *be* a mistake. At the deepest core of our being, God loves us unconditionally.

Mistakes are not a problem to God. They are only problematic for us. But they don't need to be. We could begin to see our mistakes more positively: as reminders that God loves us no matter what. Our mistakes, instead of leading us to mentally tear ourselves down, can become opportunities to learn and to lean on God.

Can we picture God saying to us, "My steadfast love will always be with you"? Do we trust that God really understands our chagrin over a failing? God understands us better than we understand ourselves, including our weaknesses and mistakes. God isn't speaking here to impossibly perfect people. It is to those of us who are struggling, the "storm-tossed," that God promises steadfast love.

Through the Day

Lord, I trust your steadfast love to cradle me through any storm.

———◇———

4 God shows his love for me every day.

"I can't understand what's going on!"

On my first visit to France, I had a wonderful time. But I was dismayed to discover how very little I remembered of my high school French. It was disorienting not to be able to understand the signs on the streets and the menus in the restaurants. As I was waiting for my flight home, there was a terrorist scare and the airport was evacuated. Hours later, when the airport reopened, I was lost in the middle of a restless crowd of hundreds of people. Directions and announcements for delayed flights were in French. I had no idea what was being said, and no one around me spoke English. Suddenly, I felt as powerless as a toddler, unable to speak, read, or understand the words being spoken.

French is not the only language I can't comprehend. God, too, sometimes speaks in a language that I don't understand. God communicates to us through our experiences in this world; they are God's love-language to us. When I become stuck in feeling bad about myself, I lose the ability to speak God's language. I see the sun shining, but I don't understand that it's shining for me. I catch a snowflake on my nose, but instead of delighting in the one-of-a-kind masterpiece of lace God has sent me, I shudder with cold. When a co-worker picks up a cup of coffee for me, I don't see that God is providing for me through the care of a friend. It's as if I have forgotten how to speak God's language—the language of love.

From God's Heart to Yours

"[Jesus] looked up and saw rich people putting their gifts into the treasury; he also saw a poor widow put in two small copper coins. He said, 'Truly I tell you, this poor widow has put in more than all of them; for all of them have contributed out of their abundance, but she out of her poverty has put in all she had to live on'" (Lk 21:1–4).

Hidden in the Darkness

In this passage from Luke, Jesus gives us a wonderful example of paying attention to the language of love.

Jesus is quite attentive to details throughout the Gospels, paying attention to things no one else notices. At this moment, Jesus could have focused on many other things besides the widow: the people who were passing the collection box without making a contribution, the hypocrisy of the wealthy who made a small contribution. But he chose to focus on the widow's seemingly insignificant offering.

Jesus doesn't just notice what the widow does, he sees the tremendous love underlying her action. Jesus understands her love for what it is.

If we pay attention to the language of love when it is spoken, we, too, can discover the underlying truth in our experiences. We begin to notice the marvelous, loving ways God speaks to us. We can allow the experience of God's unconditional love for us to touch us deeply and transform how we see ourselves and our lives.

The signs of God's love for us *are* all around us. But we often fail to see them, or when we do see them, we fail to recognize in them God's loving hand.

If we can open ourselves to God's message of love today, we can gradually grow into believing in God's love for us every day.

Through the Day

Lord, surprise me today with a sign of your steadfast love.

---

5 God lovingly provides for all my needs.

"I have nothing left to give."

Intelligent and hard-working, Robert was laid off from his job two years ago and has been unable to find work within his field. After six months of being out of work, Robert's self-confidence dropped to an all-time low. He strained to connect with his wife, who was understandably worried about their future, and the tension in their relationship carried over to the kids.

Gradually, Robert began to see how his previous scramble for success at work and his obsession to find a new job prevented him from spending time with his family. He realized that he needed to reset his priorities and focus less on his fruitless but frantic job search. Robert took a "filler job," a position way below his abilities, to help pay the bills and as an alternative to unproductive interviews. He took a night class to stay updated in his field, and became better prepared for and more selective of job interviews.

Despite all he has learned and the positive steps he has taken, Robert is now becoming desperate. He's even begged God for a job. Providing for his family means everything to him. Deep down, he feels he's failing his family. Yet Robert's persistent, desperate prayers to God seem to go unanswered.

From God's Heart to Yours

"My God, my God, why have you forsaken me? Why are you so far from helping me, from the words of my groaning? / O my God, I cry by day, but you do not answer; and by night, but find no rest" (Ps 22:1–2).

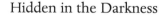

Hidden in the Darkness

This passage from Psalm 22 eloquently describes the feeling of being abandoned, of asking for help and not

receiving it. When people are deprived of what they need over a period of time—whether it's a job, a home, acceptance, or love—low self-esteem can easily develop or resurface. When our needs go unmet (including our need to provide for our loved ones), we can become ashamed of having the need in the first place. We can turn on ourselves, blaming ourselves simply for being human and having needs. Though it can be distressing, having unfulfilled needs is part of being human. We can recognize and affirm the validity of our needs by becoming proactive in seeking to fulfill them, as Robert has.

But when our efforts to meet our needs don't pay off and we feel stuck in a situation where even our prayers seem unanswered, our thirst for reassurance can seem insatiable. One prayer, one encounter with Scripture, one moment of connection with someone else, is not enough. Just as daily prayer helps develop our relationship with God, so repeated reassurance helps us grow in true self-acceptance. Instead of blaming ourselves for our needs, we can provide ourselves with some reassurance by acknowledging our needs and then entrusting our neediness to God.

On the cross, Jesus uses the words of Psalm 22 to entrust himself into the loving hands of the Father. If we, too, can entrust our very neediness to God, we will discover that God's love for us *can become* enough. When we understand that God's love embraces us—circling, sustaining, cradling us—we can then use our God-given abilities to trustfully take the steps toward the resources God lovingly provides for our needs.

Ultimately, as Saint Augustine reminds us, our hearts are made for the Eternal and will only be satisfied in God. God is the only "Enough" who not only provides for our deepest needs, but also does so in ways beyond our imagining.

Through the Day

My God, I thirst for you.

———◦———

6 In God's eyes, I am worthy.

"I don't feel worthy."

I suppose entering a convent can seem like a heroic act. But for me, it was much simpler—I fell in love with Christ and followed my deepest joy. Entering the Daughters of Saint Paul may have been a bit scary at first, but my newfound enthusiasm carried me through the initial adjustments.

After a year or so, however, I started to feel like I didn't measure up to the talented, courageous, energetic women I shared daily life with. I felt awkward, shy, inexperienced, and anxious, and made way too many mistakes. I didn't seem to have anything worthwhile to offer to God. What clinched it for me was how intimidated I felt by the patron of my community, Saint Paul. My joy in my newfound vocation disappeared. I couldn't eat, couldn't sleep, and waited miserably for the postulant director to tell me I wasn't worthy.

But she didn't. She had, however, noticed how miserable I'd become and asked me about it. So I shared my fears with her, and waited breathlessly. Would she agree? She was quiet for a moment, then asked, "Do you think Saint Paul or any of the sisters felt worthy of being called to live and communicate Christ?"

"Of course!" I replied.

She shook her head. "You really need to get to know Saint Paul," she replied. "He's not our patron because he was a success. He suffered and failed a lot. Read his letters, and discover who Saint Paul really was."

From God's Heart to Yours

"For I am the least of the apostles, unfit to be called an apostle, because I persecuted the church of God. But by the grace of God I am what I am, and his grace toward me has not been in vain" (1 Cor 15:9–10).

Hidden in the Darkness

All of us—even great saints—have reasons to feel inadequate. I'd thought Saint Paul was someone to admire from a distance. Apostle, New Testament author, and martyr, Saint Paul towered above me, stern and inaccessible. How much further could anyone possibly be from someone like me?

Yet a deeper reading of Saint Paul's letters reveals a very human character who struggled with flaws and guilt. Paul didn't just criticize the early Christians before his conversion. He actually witnessed and approved Saint Stephen's murder. How did Paul ever overcome the guilt and shame of persecuting the followers of his Lord and Savior? The secret of Paul's holiness, like that of any saint, was not in his greatness, but in God's merciful love.

And this needs to be our secret, too. Our feelings of inadequacy can make us forget that being called is not about being worthy. It is about being loved.

None of us is worthy of our sacred baptismal vocation to be Christ for others. Whatever our vocation, whether it is to give our spouse and children a foundational experience of unconditional love, or to dedicate ourselves single-heartedly to promoting the dignity of human life, or to serve in ministry, each of us is called by God to do something unique with our lives and gifts. We don't need to worry about feeling worthy, or to compare ourselves to others. We simply need to acknowledge who has called us, and trust in the power of Christ's grace and mercy working in us.

Through the Day

Lord, I believe in you, and in your power at work in me, which can do more than I could ever imagine (cf. Eph 3:20).

————◦————

7 I trust in the ways God works in my life.

"It's all up to me!"

One of my favorite ways to pray is to take a walk through the beautiful woods of New England. Once in the early quiet of morning, I turned a corner and surprised a young raccoon only ten feet or so away from me. I never saw a raccoon move so fast. It scrambled for the nearest tree—a young maple sapling—but it was going too fast. About three feet up, the raccoon lost its grip. Instead of falling flat on its back, though, the raccoon flipped upside down midair and landed on its feet. Instantly it jumped up and once again scrambled up the slender trunk. This time it succeeded, stopping perilously near the wavering treetop to look down at me.

I'm afraid I didn't give the poor animal much reassurance. I giggled at how funny it had looked as it tried too hard, too fast, to clamber up that little sapling that led nowhere. As I slowly walked away, I realized how much that raccoon reminds me of myself—when I try too hard.

From God's Heart to Yours

"Unless the LORD builds the house, those who build it labor in vain. / Unless the LORD guards the city, the guard keeps watch in vain. / It is in vain that you rise up early and go late to rest, / eating the bread of anxious toil; for he gives sleep to his beloved" (Ps 127:1–2).

Hidden in the Darkness

Psalm 127 reminds us of an important truth: while what we do is important, the results of our efforts are not up to us; they are up to God. God has a plan for us and is always working for our good. But we often forget this. We can even try to shore up our fragile sense of self by trying to prove ourselves through our achievements.

When we are trying to prove ourselves, we can often put too much importance on the results of what we are doing. We either try too hard, seeking to control the results of our efforts, or we make choices according to our need to "look good" rather than what would really be best in the situation.

Trying to prove ourselves is also spiritually unhealthy because we are basing our relationship with God and our self-worth on something changeable. However outstanding an accomplishment may be, it is never enough to permanently boost our self-esteem. In addition, no matter how much we achieve, we will always have some failures. Our sense of self-worth can end up swinging up and down dramatically according to the results of our latest project, instead of being based on our identity.

Our essential identity—that we are human beings lovingly created in the image of God—never changes. Our choices and actions don't change this core identity, but can express, strengthen, and develop it. When we begin to trust in God's love for us, we can also trust the results of our efforts to his loving care, knowing that God's plan for us is better than anything we could come up with. We no longer need to be caught in a frantic, restless need to prove our self-worth, but can act out of a sense of security and peace.

Through the Day

Jesus, I entrust the results of my efforts to you.

———◦———

8 God wants my deepest happiness.

"What if I don't deserve to be happy?"

In the beginning of George Eliot's novel *Middlemarch*, young and inexperienced Dorothea Brooke is desperate for a purpose in life that will give her some sense of self-worth. She naively decides to settle for marriage to a much older, scholarly bachelor, not for love but solely to assist him in his obscure but seemingly important research.

Dorothea is quickly disillusioned when her husband only tolerates her assistance and offers little in the way of tenderness or companionship. As her sense of purpose-lessness grows, she even questions the importance of his research. Fortunately for Dorothea and the readers, this is not the end of the story. Dorothea's experience teaches her to value herself, and that enables her to begin to shape her life in a way more in tune with her deeper desires.

Our society contrasts greatly with the Victorian society depicted in the novel, but Dorothea's problem remains quite common. When we suffer from low self-esteem, we often settle for something less, because unconsciously we don't think we deserve to be truly happy.

From God's Heart to Yours

"You show me the path of life. In your presence there is fullness of joy; in your right hand are pleasures forevermore" (Ps 16:11).

Hidden in the Darkness

The insights of Psalm 16 show that true happiness goes far beyond a particular moment, situation, or possession. Happiness is a joyful fullness, a journeying on the path of life. Today, perhaps we would describe happiness as living a full life.

Every person desires and deserves a full life, and this is God's desire for each person, too. Living life fully includes living our potential and undergoing the full range of human emotions and experiences. So the path to happiness does not exclude all suffering. The greatest joys of life—such as loving another person—carry within them the greatest pains as well. (For example, if we love someone, we risk the pain of loss and separation.) It's hard for us to accept suffering as a part of life, and it's even harder when suffering blots out our sense of joy entirely. We might begin to think of life in terms of surviving, of avoiding the next disaster, or of simply being a notch less miserable. "Life" is reduced to survival. "Happiness" is limited to suffering less. But this is not the fullness of life and happiness God wants for us.

We may even be tempted to think that God doesn't want us to be happy, or that we don't deserve to be happy. This false death of hope intensifies our suffering. Instead, God's desire is to give us the kind of happiness described in Psalm 16.

The question becomes: How can we trust in God's desire for us?

We can begin by focusing on the giftedness of our lives, recognizing the many ways in which God provides for us, even when we are suffering. Gratitude opens us to the possibilities offered by God. God wants to save us so that we can live fully and deeply. God wants us to grow into a deep fulfillment, into possessing a profound understanding of our value and place in the world, into making our lives a loving gift of ourselves to others, into sharing our gifts with the world in the way only we can.

In our prayers, let us share our deepest desires with God, and let us be open to God's deep desires for us.

Through the Day

Lord, I trust in your desire for my happiness.

———◦———

9 God wants to speak heart to heart with me.

"God, how could you do this to me?"

Inez divorced her husband several years after their marriage because of his infidelity. She struggled to accept that, as a Catholic, she could never marry again.

One night just after the divorce had gone through, Inez needed to talk to her ex-husband about their four-year-old son. When she called him, a woman answered the phone. Devastated, Inez slammed down the phone and ran to her son's bedroom, where he was sleeping soundly. Sitting on his bed, she lashed out silently at God. "How could you do this to me? I don't believe you are there anymore. I'm leaving you if you don't show me your love right now!"

Just then, her son restlessly turned over. As he did, he moved his arm and his hand slapped her on the chin. Stunned, she realized that God had answered her! In a moment, her anger changed to gratitude. "Lord, if this is the love you're showing me right now, in my son, that's enough. Thank you for the gift of his life—your greatest gift to me."

Inez went to confession and told the priest she had been angry with God and had threatened to give up on God and stop believing in him. The priest laughed and told her, "You were simply being honest about your feelings. It's wonderful that you have such a real relationship with God."

Inez still draws strength from the memory of her son's unintentional slap on the chin—a powerful reminder of God's faithful love.

From God's Heart to Yours

"Trust in him at all times, O people; pour out your heart before him; God is a refuge for us" (Ps 62:8).

Hidden in the Darkness

The psalms show us that praying is more than reciting the prayers we memorized as children. Whatever we are feeling, we can find in the psalms—the most honest and heartfelt of prayers. But some of us never read the "messy" psalms: the ones that complain, lament, or beg God to take action.

In inspiring the psalms, the Holy Spirit may have been giving us a clue about how God wants to relate to us. So many times, we think our prayers have to come from the best part of ourselves—the part of us that is *not* angry or jealous or fearful. But God wants our prayer to come from our entire being. God wants us to share everything with him, every experience. "Pour out your heart to me," God begs us. "Trust me with your deepest feelings and needs, with your heartbreaks and your joys. Don't ever think that you are alone. I am with you."

Jesus gives us another clue about prayer with the parable of the Pharisee and the tax-collector. The tax-collector
doesn't use fancy words; he is just honest about who he
really is: "God, be merciful to me, a sinner!" (cf. Lk 18:9–
14) As we read the Gospels attentively, we will notice that,
in his interactions with people, Jesus responds most open-
ly to honesty. Even when people challenge him, Jesus
seems to value most those who speak from their hearts.

If we speak to God honestly from our heart, even if it's
just a quick prayer, God cannot resist responding. Our
prayer becomes a holy and intimate dialogue: from our
heart to God's, and from God's heart to ours.

Through the Day

God, I open my heart to you and invite you in.

———◁○▷———

10 God lovingly provides for me in every circumstance.

"God asks too many sacrifices!"

Matt is a young man with a future full of possibilities.
On track for a successful business career, Matt is physically fit and enthusiastically lives his faith in his parish and
with the youth group he leads.

But lately, Matt has been troubled, sensing that something is missing from his life. At first, he thought it was

because he isn't currently dating. But then the parish priest suggested to Matt that he might be called to the priesthood.

Though Matt values the priesthood, he had never considered becoming a priest himself—it always seemed too hard. Yet, Matt is now starting to wonder whether he should try for the priesthood. He feels attracted to the idea, but is afraid he wouldn't be able to bear the sacrifices involved.

From God's Heart to Yours

"If God is for us, who is against us? He who did not withhold his own Son, but gave him up for all of us, will he not with him also give us everything else?" (Rom 8:31–32)

Hidden in the Darkness

Romans 8 is one of the most eloquent passages in the Letters of Saint Paul. In this chapter (and the previous one), Paul seeks to unpack the consequences of salvation —unimaginable, too-good-to-be-true consequences! For Paul, God is the Father who gives his own beloved Son for our sake. Jesus, the beloved Son, lovingly pours himself out for us that we may share in God's very life for all eternity. Through Jesus, there is nothing that we cannot claim as our own. We share in the very Sonship of Jesus. "Joint heirs with Christ" is how Paul puts it a few verses earlier.

If Jesus truly wants to give us "everything else," then the sacrifices of our vocation are not about God wanting to strip us bare. They are about *receiving*.

For example, the celibacy a priest chooses has a sacrificial aspect, but it is really a gift meant to open his heart to receive and share Jesus' love more freely. By choosing an exclusive relationship with Christ and the Church over having his own family, a priest frees his heart to serve lovingly whoever needs him. In marriage, each spouse's exclusive fidelity enriches and deepens the couple's love so that it becomes a constant source of life, joy, and self-giving.

In every choice we make, we let go of something in order to receive what we think is better for us. God's plan includes some sacrifices, but we receive so much more. And the sacrifices we will be called to make will never be more than we can bear, because God is with us and will give us what we need.

Those moments when we are stuck in seeing only the sacrifices of our life (or fear of future sacrifices), we can step back and look at the bigger picture by asking ourselves, "How is God providing for me today? What gift is God offering me in this situation?"

Through the Day

Jesus, my Good Shepherd, today I open my eyes and heart to the ways you lovingly provide for me.

―――◄○►―――

11 No worry or fear can separate me from God's love.

"I just can't stop worrying about it."

I am such a worrier. I even used to fret that my worrying meant I didn't trust enough in God. If I truly trusted God, I wouldn't worry at all, right? Fortunately, I discovered an elderly sister of my community, Sister Mary Attilia, who shared the same tendency to worry. She was a gentle soul with such a great sense of humor that at first I didn't recognize how anxious she was. Her worries were different from mine, however: I worried mostly about myself, while she worried mostly about others.

I got to know Sister Mary Attilia well during the last years of her life, when she was gradually losing her health, the ability to do what she loved, and her stubborn independence. She took great comfort in prayer, but sometimes her anxiety would overwhelm her, and then the best I could do was to tease her (it always worked!) and spend time with her.

In her last weeks, I witnessed a miracle in this woman who had spent her life doing for and worrying about everyone else. God worked in her so gently, so marvelously, that she simply let go of all her anxieties. She surrendered everything. In her last lucid moments, she told one of the sisters, "I think the Father is calling me." From that moment on, she simply rested in the hands of God until he carried her home.

Witnessing firsthand how tenderly God acted with

Sister Mary Attilia changed my life. My worries might
stop me from *feeling* loved by God, but nothing, not even
my darkest fears, can prevent my faithful God from tenderly caring for me.

From God's Heart to Yours

*"For I am convinced that neither death, nor life, nor
angels, nor rulers, nor things present, nor things to
come, nor powers, nor height, nor depth, nor anything
else in all creation, will be able to separate us from the
love of God in Christ Jesus our Lord" (Rom 8:38–39).*

Hidden in the Darkness

When we are anxious, we experience life as a series of
obstacles or blocks. But what if we really believed this
exultant conclusion of Saint Paul's hymn to God's love?
What if life were not a series of obstacles, but a series of
opportunities through which we discover anew God's
faithful love for us?

A diamond ring is the tangible pledge of faithful, life-
long love that a man traditionally offers to his fiancée,
because a diamond is indestructible, multifaceted, endur-
ing, and radiant. The diamond of our faith, the tangible
pledge of God's ever-faithful love for us, is the Mass, the
Eucharistic Celebration.

At the center of every Eucharistic Celebration, at the
consecration of the bread and wine into Jesus' Body and

Blood, we witness Jesus offering himself completely to the Father for us. Not only does Jesus offer himself *for* us, but he offers himself *to* us, inviting us to receive him in Communion so that we can be more fully united to him.

Whenever doubts arise about whether God loves us, or we start to worry, we can simply gaze in wonder at the diamond God has given us: stop by a church for a visit, say a prayer to Jesus in the Eucharist, or simply consider God's self-giving love, which we witness every time we go to Mass.

Through the Day

Eucharistic Jesus, Radiant Presence of God's unbounded love, I trust in you.

————◄○►————

12 God lovingly chose to create me.

"I am not good enough."

For a time during grade school I didn't fit in. As a third grader, I blamed it on a litany of reasons: I didn't misbehave or take risks because being punished was so boring; my parents didn't allow me to watch popular TV shows; I could never stay for after-school activities... For whatever reason, having no friends lasted for two years.

Two years is a long time for a kid to feel friendless. It's a long time to be alone in the schoolyard during recess, and an even longer time to have no one to sit with at lunchtime. I began to think there was something wrong with me—maybe I wasn't "good enough" to have a friend.

Surprisingly, after the bouts of embarrassment and loneliness eased, I started to enjoy having quiet time—a rarity at home. I didn't have to force myself to fit in. I even started to worry less about what the other kids thought. Then, at the beginning of fifth grade, the new girl who joined our class became my first-ever best friend.

External circumstances, especially the ways others react to us, can make us question our own value. We need to base our sense of self-worth on something more permanent.

From God's Heart to Yours

"[Y]ou knit me together in my mother's womb. / I praise you, for I am fearfully and wonderfully made" (Ps 139:13–14).

Hidden in the Darkness

There is one truth that cannot be twisted no matter how much our wounded nature might try. This truth is that God chose to create each of us. There is something so unique and wonderful about us and it is this: God wants to share his life with us. God wants us in the world.

Many of us are convinced deep down that we are no good, or that there is something fundamentally wrong with us. When we feel rejected, our fragile self-esteem can plummet. Yet, our faith tells us that since God our Creator is all-wise and all-good, he must have good reasons to create us as we are, with our personalities and our potentials. The reality that God lovingly created us and sustains us is bedrock upon which we can build a new foundation for a positive sense of self-worth.

The Father wasn't careless about making us. The psalmist poetically describes how we are knit together by God—every strand of us woven into a beautiful whole. So often we focus on just a part of ourselves: our weaknesses or what we lack. Instead, Psalm 139 encourages us to look at our whole selves with new eyes, from the miracle of our bodies to the most amazing gifts of all—our intellect and our free will, especially the ability to love. Our intelligence and freedom enable us to shape our own lives and to influence the lives of those around us.

We are all created in God's image, but how we reflect God to the world is according to our unique combination of gifts. A lifetime is not long enough to discover and develop every gift we have received. Only recently have I started to suspect that during my "friendless" grade school years I was developing a gift: a love of solitude.

Psalm 139 can lead us into amazement and awe over how wonderfully God has made us. We can make a list of God's gifts to us, and then pick a different gift to thank God for each day.

Through the Day

Loving Creator, thank you for loving me into being.

---◀◦▶---

13 God invites me to accept myself as I am.

"Admitting my faults just makes me feel worse."

Mark is a dedicated father, husband, and veteran cop. Over the years, his wife has tried to tell him that his outbursts of temper are getting worse, but Mark won't listen. He doesn't think he loses his temper that often, only when his job is stressful.

Finally, when building a tree house for the kids during summer vacation, Mark explodes. He smashes the hammer into a pile of boards, scattering them over the ground. He looks up to see his two children frozen where they stand. The fear in his daughter's eyes pierces through his denials.

That evening, Mark begins talking with his wife about how to deal with his temper.

Honestly admitting our faults might be uncomfortable, but it's the only way we can begin to change.

From God's Heart to Yours

"[W]hat does the LORD require of you / but to do justice, and to love kindness, and to walk humbly with your God?" (Mic 6:8)

Hidden in the Darkness

This oft-quoted passage from the prophet Micah challenges how we think about being humble. Humility, arguably the most misunderstood virtue of the Christian life, doesn't mean being miserably down on ourselves. "Walking humbly" doesn't mean shuffling along bent over, weighed down by a lifetime of guilt. Micah puts humility—being self-aware and truthful with ourselves— into its proper context of our relationships with God and with others.

To be humble means: 1) to know and accept who we really are, 2) to acknowledge our utter dependence on God, and 3) to be responsible for our choices and actions, striving to be fair and kind both to ourselves and others. In essence, humility is to be in right relationship with ourselves, God, and others.

Growing in self-awareness is an important part of humility. A spiritual practice called the examen of consciousness is one way that we can become more self-aware. Entire books have been written about how to make this deeply fruitful spiritual practice, and I've recommended some in the list of resources at the end of this book. But anyone can begin making the examen of consciousness because it is simply taking a deeper look at our own life.

In the examen, we prayerfully go back over the events of our day, looking at both the graces we received and how we responded to them. Increasingly aware of the ways God works in our life and in the choices we make, we gradually begin to live more reflectively, with greater self-awareness.

For many of us, though, the most difficult aspect of humility is to accept the faults that we become aware of in ourselves. Accepting our faults doesn't mean that we like them, but that we acknowledge what we said, what we did, or what we neglected to do. If we don't acknowledge our faults, we can't change them. When we take responsibility for our choices, we can decide to make amends for whatever we did in the past, and do things differently in the future. As Catholics, we have the advantage of the gift of the Sacrament of Reconciliation to help us.

Humility is truth—the *whole truth*—about us. God knows us through and through, and loves us as we are. Yet God is also always inviting us to become our best selves. We can learn to accept ourselves as we are, while acknowledging the areas in which we need to grow.

Through the Day

Jesus, in your love, reassure me today that I am more than just my faults.

———◦———

14 God calls me to live in love.

"I am so sick of being me. I hate myself!"

Self-hate used to flare up pretty often for me, especially when I blamed myself for something. It was deeply painful not to be at peace with myself. I started to question whether I'd *ever* be able to rise above it.

I vividly remember the first time I made a mistake and realized that I wasn't upset about it. Curiously, I examined my feelings. I discovered I felt sympathy for myself instead of guilt! What a relief to understand that I had, for once, avoided falling into the trap of self-hate.

For a moment, the earth felt a bit unsteady under my feet—or was it my legs that were unsteady? And something inside of me shifted, too, as I caught a glimpse of a hope-filled future: What if, instead of tearing myself down, I could be my own support and source of encouragement?

My efforts to be kinder to myself were finally—if unexpectedly—bearing fruit.

From God's Heart to Yours

"I pray that, according to the riches of his glory, he may grant that you may be strengthened in your inner being with power through his Spirit, and that Christ may dwell in your hearts through faith, as you are being rooted and grounded in love" (Eph 3:16–17).

Hidden in the Darkness

As Christians, we often hear the command to love God and to love others, and we might think (as I did) that we can do this somehow—or we are supposed to do this—by disregarding ourselves. But as this passage from Ephesians makes clear, authentic love is rooted in a clear sense of identity and a healthy self-regard: an "inner being" strengthened in the Spirit and rooted in love. If we don't have these, then our neediness—for survival, for self-defense, for love and acceptance—will take over, and our love will not be genuine.

Loving self doesn't mean that we are blind to our faults, but that we accept ourselves as we have been created by God, and we take care of ourselves with gentleness and compassion.

If we place this prayer from Ephesians next to the tenets of self-hate, the contrast is startling. Many of us have some experience with self-hate, but an attitude or habit of self-hatred is a torment that leeches away our inner peace and hope. We become unable to recognize God's goodness to us or in us, unable to know or see ourselves for who we are, and we remain trapped in a painful cycle of unfairly blaming ourselves for anything that goes wrong.

Without a healthy self-love, the command of Jesus to love our neighbors as ourselves makes no sense at all. Self-hatred prevents us not only from receiving God's love in its fullness, but also from fully living our unique calling. It makes sense that, if God wants us to be a source of peace and love for others, God must also want us to accept and love ourselves for who we are. God calls us to be rooted in love, and this includes a healthy love of self.

We can begin to genuinely love ourselves by being gentle with ourselves and trying to see ourselves through God's eyes. As we come to understand our identity—created and loved by God, chosen to be Christ's dwelling place *and* for a particular mission of service—we discover that we are indeed lovable.

Through the Day

Jesus, Gentle Master, dwell in me and teach me to see myself through your loving eyes.

———◦———

15 God rejoices when I seek forgiveness.

"I don't deserve to be forgiven."

Recently, I made a thoughtless remark and really hurt the feelings of someone with whom I work closely. I did not even realize what I had said until she repeated it back to me, and then I felt awful. My unkind words reflected how completely self-absorbed I'd been.

Immediately, I asked for my co-worker's forgiveness. But even though she said, "It's okay," I went through the rest of the day with a sense of shame. I kept wondering if she had *really* forgiven me.

How hard it can be for me to accept forgiveness! When I get to the point of acknowledging a fault, guilt is the appropriate response, but instead I can become lost in shame. Guilt acknowledges the sinful action and seeks to make amends. Shame, instead, turns inward and deci-mates my sense of self-worth. Then, even though the other person forgives me, I can't accept that grace because I don't feel that I deserve to be forgiven. I become trapped in the hopelessness of shame.

From God's Heart to Yours

"[L]et us eat and celebrate; for this son of mine was dead and is alive again; he was lost and is found!" (Lk 15:23–24)

Hidden in the Darkness

All of us feel a need for forgiveness at some time. Forgiveness is an important part of any relationship, because all of us are limited; we make mistakes and sinful choices.

The Scripture quotation is from the parable of the Prodigal Son—the father's words of rejoicing as he embraces his just-returned child. You may want to stop now and read the entire parable in Luke 15:11–32.

In the parable of the Prodigal Son, as well as the other parables in chapter 15 of the Gospel of Luke, God has a strikingly different perspective on forgiveness from ours. These parables shift the focus away from the shame of the sinner onto God's eagerness and joy in granting mercy. The woman who finds the coin, the shepherd who finds the sheep, the father of the prodigal son—each rejoices beyond all expectation in their reunions. Why is this?

What might Jesus be trying to tell us through these parables?

God knows us better than we know ourselves, even how prone we are to sin. And God laments each of our sins. Yet for God, sin, guilt, and shame are not the last words. God offers us the graced healing of forgiveness through the Sacrament of Reconciliation. This sacrament goes by many names. "Confession" focuses on the telling of our sins to the priest. "Penance" focuses on the penitential aspect of the sacrament. By any name, the Sacrament of Reconciliation is a celebration of God's loving and inexhaustible mercy, and a renewal of our relationship with God.

Every time we admit our sins and ask God for forgiveness, God is delighted. In the ocean of God's mercy, our shame and sinfulness become insignificant, washed away. God never tires of bringing us new life! And each time we become more aware of our sinfulness and seek forgiveness, we have an opportunity to grow closer to God.

The Church, inspired by the Spirit, invites us to receive the Sacrament of Reconciliation often. We *never* need to be afraid to ask God to forgive us … again. We delight God each time we seek to be more deeply united with him.

Through the Day

Lord, draw me close to you.

———◦———

16 I remember how blessed I am.

"Everything is going wrong!"

At the end of the 1998 swashbuckler film *The Man in the Iron Mask*, one of the main characters, the Musketeer d'Artagnan, meets his grown son for the first time—a son he never knew existed. They literally have only moments before they face death—not even time for one embrace. Yet in his last few seconds of life, d'Artagnan's attitude is remarkable. Rather than mourn the untimeliness of his death, he is instead incredibly grateful at how he is dying —with his newly discovered son and comrades at his side.

I was deeply struck by d'Artagnan's reaction because, even though he knew he would die, his last moments were blessed with an intimacy and love that he never would have experienced if he had focused on his pain and loss. By living the gift of his last moments so fully, d'Artagnan was also able to give a tremendous gift to his son in the few moments they shared.

Like most people, when something goes wrong, I am tempted to focus on the unpleasant or difficult consequences. When I do that, I risk missing the grace or blessing hidden in the moment. Like d'Artagnan, I want to recognize and accept the giftedness of each moment.

From God's Heart to Yours

"It is good to give thanks to the LORD, to sing praises to your name, O Most High; / to declare your steadfast

love in the morning, and your faithfulness by night …
at the works of your hands I sing for joy" (Ps 92:1–2).

Hidden in the Darkness

Living in a spirit of thanksgiving is not easy when we are suffering. Because life is full of both pain and joy, we often have to work at cultivating a grateful heart. The psalms, like life, are also interwoven with pain, fear, joy, and thanksgiving. The beauty of praying the psalms regularly is that we begin to share the psalmist's understanding that God wants to be involved in every moment of our lives—the sufferings, the joys, the failures, the victories. Praying the psalms regularly can help us to see our lives with new eyes.

For those of us struggling with any kind of deep pain, including low self-esteem or self-hatred, life can sometimes seem to be more of a burden than a gift. But we cannot let this distorted perception guide our choices. That we exist, are self-aware, can make choices, and experience love, joy, and pain—all of these are pure gift. Painful times contain hidden blessings if we have eyes to see and hearts open to receive. Even on the most difficult of days, God sustains us with air to breathe, ground to stand on, sky to look up into, family and friends to lean on…. When we recognize the countless ways God blesses us, we daily discover anew how tremendously he loves us.

Learning to live with a grateful heart means changing perspective. Inspired by Psalm 92, we can decide each morning to look for that day's blessings, and at the end of the day to write down five things we are grateful for. My daily list mixes the simplest things, like "a good cup of coffee," with the most cherished gifts, such as, "my mom's love for me."

As we practice becoming fully aware of the gift of each moment, our joy and awareness of God's loving care for us deepens too.

Through the Day

Lord, thank you for crowning me with your love today by...

————◆————

17 God's love is my security.

"I've got to prove myself!"

Arthur's computer has a 21-inch plasma screen, extra memory, and the latest video card. He crams online gaming into every available moment, and lately he's spending so much time online that he's started to neglect his family, his friends, and commitments he's made. Arthur's frequent late-night gaming is even starting to affect his efficiency at work.

But when he's gaming, Arthur is totally enthralled. He likes feeling that he is a hero who makes a difference, and the game constantly offers him new challenges to overcome and an increased sense of accomplishment when he succeeds. Unfortunately though, Arthur is allowing the game to pull him away from engaging in his real life.

Many activities can become obsessive or even addicting because of the easy good feelings or sense of accomplishment they offer. Gamers can crave the sense of accomplishment that proficiency in the game brings. (Proficiency in an online game is a skill that may take effort and practice to achieve, but it's not the same kind of accomplishment as achieving a goal in life.) These feelings can satisfy us superficially, but they can't replace relationships or real accomplishments.

A genuine sense of accomplishment can be a healthy way to build self-confidence in our abilities. But no matter how great our accomplishments, we can't rely on them to prove our self-worth. None of us needs to do this. The need to prove ourselves is motivated by the fear that we are not good enough or lovable as we are.

From God's Heart to Yours

"[P]erfect love casts out fear.... We love because [God] first loved us" (1 Jn 4:18–19).

Hidden in the Darkness

John's letter offers us an alternative to the need to prove ourselves: instead of focusing on ourselves, focus on God's love for us.

When we feel we need to prove ourselves, we are caught in a self-defeating and never-ending circle. We become self-absorbed and are distracted from the real purpose of our lives. We are driven by the fear of not being good enough in our own eyes, in the eyes of others, or perhaps even in the eyes of God. Defensive and fearful, we can turn in on ourselves, seeing only our own trivial concerns or seeking superficial reassurance in how much we accomplish. However, we can let go of this urgent need to prove ourselves when we allow the light of God's love to permeate our lives.

Allowing Jesus to become our security is a gradual process, but it is deeply joyful and freeing. The very foundation of our identity shifts, so that God's love for us and our love for God become the source of all our thoughts and actions.

Although we don't need to prove ourselves to God, our choices and actions are far from meaningless. Rediscovering and focusing on God's love frees us from fear and the need to prove ourselves. God's love empowers us to begin to share our joy and life in Christ with others. Each time we choose to act for the love of God, self, or neighbor, we take a step away from being controlled by fear and a step toward greater love and freedom. Healthy self-esteem is reinforced when our choices reflect our convictions rather than our fear of the opinions of others.

Saint Augustine says, "Love, and do what you want." Truly, love is the most powerful and joyful motivation on earth.

Through the Day

Lord Jesus, fill me with your Spirit of love, power, and joy.

———◄○►———

18 God's love is a never-ending stream flowing through my life.

"I'm back to hating myself again."

Life's pressures really challenge me to maintain a God-centered perspective that includes my place in God's loving arms.

A while ago, I had a stressful week. I felt completely overwhelmed. A co-worker's criticism, a particularly daunting task that didn't go well, and my disappointment all conspired to trigger a self-defeating attitude. I tried to bury myself in work, but by the end of the week I realized that I was carrying an immensely heavier burden than my usual workload: I was back to hating myself.

I felt trapped. In my prayer, God seemed a faraway judge rather than a loving Creator, and I couldn't connect with a sense of Jesus' merciful love, either. I began to obsess about my faults and started blaming myself just for feeling stressed.

Finally, it got to be too much. Intuitively, I decided to give myself a chance to relax. I went to one of my favorite places in the city of Toronto—a narrow park that borders the Humber River—and sat for a long time under a graciously curved willow that leans over the river. As I sat there, hidden behind a screen of whispering leaves, my inner chaos gradually subsided.

By my taking a break and opening to the beauty of nature—something I really enjoyed—the negative thought pattern was disrupted long enough for me to evaluate it and let it go.

From God's Heart to Yours

"Blessed are those who trust in the LORD, whose trust is the LORD. / They shall be like a tree planted by water, sending out its roots by the stream" (Jer 17:7–8).

Hidden in the Darkness

Willows need lots of moisture and are often planted near plentiful sources of water. This passage from Jeremiah not only brings to mind lovely willow trees bending over the Humber River, but it also reminds us that we need to choose well where we "plant" ourselves, where we dig deep and send out our roots.

We can choose to be rooted in the desert of life's hardships, or in our own failures and negativity. But when we root ourselves in the arid desert, it is much harder for us to grow or bear fruit. We become brittle and parched, like a dried-out shrub.

We can also choose to be rooted in God's love. A stream is a great image of God's love, because God's love is not a one-time privilege to be earned but is always available to us, ever-flowing through the minutes of our days and of our lives, never running out. Even in great loss (imagine a branch chopped off the tree), we can still drink in God's love so we can heal, grow, and thrive.

Life is a thirsty business. It demands a lot of us. But God's love is always there to refresh and renew us. No matter what challenge we face, God is lovingly present with us *in* that challenge.

One way to root ourselves deeply in God's love for us is to read the Word of God often. The Scriptures constantly remind us of who God is and who we are to God. Paradoxically, the harder it is for us to believe that we are loved, the more important it is for us to remember: we are loved tenderly.

Through the Day

My God, today I renew my belief and my joy in your love for me!

———◄○►———

PART 2

SHAPING MY IDENTITY
IN CHRIST

19 My hopes and disappointments open my heart to the blessings of God.

"I can't bear to be disappointed!"

As a child I learned not to set my heart on anything for fear of being disappointed. I have since tried to open myself to anticipation, sometimes successfully. Vacation is one of the things that I let myself build up hopes for—I am rarely disappointed.

A couple of years ago, I managed to juggle the gaps in my own various commitments with a friend's crowded schedule to arrange a week of vacation together at a rarely available beach house. Several days beforehand, my friend suddenly canceled on me. I was angry, hurt, and bitterly disappointed, especially because it was impossible to reschedule.

Disappointment is difficult for me because it's so painful to accept that I can't have what I've counted on. The many other feelings that accompany disappointments —such as anger, sadness, betrayal, and hopelessness— make disappointment even harder to handle.

I know now that squelching hope isn't the answer, because it denies the goodness of life and closes me to unexpected joys. But I'm still tempted at times to avoid hoping, just so I won't have to bear the pain of disappointment.

From God's Heart to Yours

"Ask, and it will be given to you; search, and you will find; knock, and the door will be opened for you.... If you ... know how to give good gifts to your children, how much more will the heavenly Father give the Holy Spirit to those who ask him!" (Lk 11:9–13)

Hidden in the Darkness

Having needs and desires is a part of being human; sharing them with another is an act of trust in the one with whom we share them. Jesus encourages us to trust God with our wants and needs because God delights in providing for us.

But just as we can be disappointed by something or someone we trust, we can also feel disappointed by God. We have all had the experience of praying for something and not receiving it. One way we can react to our disappointment is to doubt that we are worth listening to. We can even twist the words of Jesus to "prove" that God isn't listening to our prayers: we asked God for something and we didn't receive it.

Going deeper into Jesus' words, we realize he *doesn't* promise that we will receive exactly what we ask for. Rather, Jesus promises that we will receive *something*—and if it's not what we asked for, it will be even better—the gift of the Spirit of God. We have every reason to hope!

God continually provides for us far beyond anything we could hope for: we just need to have eyes and hearts open to receive God's blessings. When we deny our hopes and desires out of fear of feeling the honest pain of disappointment, we may become closed or sour, not ready to accept the unexpected gifts that God wants to give us.

The anger and hurt that accompany disappointment may be hard to cope with initially, but we don't want to close ourselves off completely from the hope that our desires will be fulfilled. Hope makes us receptive. Unfulfilled longings can remind us that we are incomplete by ourselves, that we need God. When we are aware of our emptiness, we have room to receive the surprises God wants to give us.

Through the Day

Lord, I wait on you to fulfill my deepest desires.

———◁◦▷———

20 God lovingly restores me to life.

"It's so hard for me to admit my sins!"

Four-year-old Harry loves swordplay. Recently, Harry's Uncle Kevin visited and became his new dueling partner. Each time Harry managed to tap him with his little blue plastic sword, towering Uncle Kevin would clutch his chest and dramatically collapse onto the sofa or the floor—or both. Moments later, they'd be at it again.

A few days after Kevin left, Harry said to his mother, "Mummy, Uncle Kevin does it better!"

His mother, six months pregnant with Harry's little sister, smiled. "What does Uncle Kevin do better?"

"Die and come back to life again!" Harry responded enthusiastically.

"Die and come back to life" is something that all of us could learn to do better. Ongoing conversion—a continual dying to ourselves and rising to new life—is a necessary part of our life in Christ. Both conversion and a healthy self-esteem begin with the choice to accept the whole truth about ourselves, including our sinfulness.

But if we are truly honest about the flaws and sins we are most ashamed of, how do we avoid becoming stuck in our shame?

From God's Heart to Yours

"Do you not know that all of us who have been baptized in Christ Jesus were baptized into his death? Therefore we have been buried with him by baptism into death, so that, just as Christ was raised from the dead by the glory of the Father, so we too might walk in newness of life" (Rom 6:3–4).

Hidden in the Darkness

In his Letter to the Romans, Saint Paul speaks about our life in Christ as a cyclical journey of dying to sin and rising to life. In Baptism, we "died to sin" and began to share in the gift of God's own life. When we sin, we need God's healing so we can once again share fully in God's life. Admitting the truth about the sins we commit is the first step that opens us to this healing.

When we are insecure about our self-worth, it can be extremely painful to see our faults clearly—a real "dying" to our illusions about ourselves. It might seem easier to try to ignore our sins, or to distract ourselves by focusing on a superficial imperfection instead. But denying the truth about our sins is an attempt at self-deception that never fully succeeds. Any denial of the truth is a betrayal of ourselves and undermines our self-esteem, because deep down, some part of us knows the truth. Denying the truth about our sinfulness is like building on sand. God invites us to build on the bedrock of truth instead.

Accepting our truth—both our belovedness and our sinfulness—is one of the most important choices we can make in our relationship with God and with ourselves. Being prone to sin is part of who we are, but God's desire to heal and forgive us is much more powerful. However, we can only experience the power of God's forgiveness when we admit what we have done and give him our woundedness.

Letting go of our illusions about ourselves leads us to growth and new life. God constantly invites us to live in peace with the full truth about who we are and how beloved we are. What if every time we sinned were not just an occasion to feel guilty, but first of all became a reminder of how much God wants to love us and restore us to the fullness of life?

Through the Day

Lord, heal me in your steadfast love!

—◦—

21 I appreciate the people God has put in my life.

"I am afraid to depend on my friends."

In the book *Anne of Green Gables*, by author L. M. Montgomery, one of newly adopted Anne Shirley's greatest hopes in her new life is to have a best friend. Orphaned as an infant, Anne has spent her childhood either in an orphanage or as the caregiver of younger children in foster homes. The only friend she has ever had was imaginary.

Normally satisfied with her appearance (except for her red hair), Anne panics about what to wear to the church picnic when she discovers that Diana—a girl who lives nearby—will be there. The desperate intensity with which Anne longs for a "best friend" is striking. For Anne, having a friend is an important sign that a whole new life is opening up for her.

But Anne's childlike intensity is accompanied by a surprisingly mature understanding of what friendship is all about. Once she and Diana become friends, Anne easily confides in and generously sympathizes with her. Instead of crippling her ability to trust, Anne's previous lack of friends enables her to appreciate Diana's friendship as an unmatchable treasure.

From God's Heart to Yours

"I have indeed received much joy and encouragement from your love, because the hearts of the saints have been refreshed through you" (Philem 1:7).

Hidden in the Darkness

Of all the writers of the New Testament, Saint Paul most often expresses his appreciation for the gift of friendship, warmly greeting numerous friends in every letter. In this quotation that opens his Letter to Philemon, Paul shares his "short list" of the gifts of friendship exemplified in Philemon: joy, encouragement, love, refreshment. What gifts do our friends bring us?

Every relationship in our life is a gift—even if it is an opportunity to practice kindness when we don't feel like it! But close friends are a special gift; they enliven us in a unique way. In Paul's words, a true friend encourages us to be our best selves and refreshes us. To be refreshed is to receive new life.

Sometimes a friend reveals God's love for us through support or encouragement. At other times, a friend reflects back God's face *in us*. Through the friend's eyes, we glimpse how God rejoices in us, works through us, or lives in us. Friendship can truly be a privileged way God acts in our lives.

When we feel more vulnerable, we may allow the fear of losing a friend we depend on to block us from beginning or deepening a close friendship. It is both possible and likely that after we have grown close to someone, we will eventually lose them in some way: either when we are geographically separated, or when we grow apart, or even when one of us dies. If we don't allow fear to block us from developing deeper friendships, we might be surprised to discover that our own emotional resilience and the gifts of the friendship itself will sustain us in the event of a loss.

Friends are a twofold gift: first, God has put them in our lives; second, the friend chooses to relate to us. The encouragement, companionship, support, and vision our friends share with us shape us and become a part of who we are. A true friend will, in some way, remain with us always.

Through the Day

Thank you, Lord, for blessing me through my friend,
_____.

◄○►

22 I entrust my burdens to Jesus.

"I feel so tired and drained."

I was once working alone on a long-term project. I gradually became obsessed with it and the need to prove myself. As weeks stretched into months and my fatigue deepened, I began to notice something strange: the colors in the world around me literally seemed to wash out. Everything was tinged with gray.

I know now that when I reach the point of exhaustion, my vision is affected—it's a physical warning that I need to slow down. But being tired didn't just dull my physical vision: it affected my spiritual perspective just as dramatically. Fatigue darkened my perceptions of myself and drained away my trust in God. The more tired I became, the more "down" on myself I became, and the less I sought the support I needed. Eventually, I started resenting my own fatigue, accusing myself of being lazy, even though I was stretched to my limits.

I eventually finished the project, but I promised myself that I would never let myself fall into that obsessive, exhausting, spirit-draining cycle again.

From God's Heart to Yours

"Come to me, all you that are weary and are carrying heavy burdens, and I will give you rest. Take my yoke

upon you, and learn from me; for I am gentle and hum-
ble in heart" (Mt 11:28–29).

Hidden in the Darkness

Fatigue is part of being human. Jesus knows all about fatigue—from his life as a manual laborer to the overwhelming demands of his public ministry. Jesus invites us to bring this very human experience of fatigue into the light of his love for us. He seems to have special concern for those who are not just suffering from physical fatigue, but who find life itself heavy. Often, it's not the amount of work or commitments we find overwhelming, but our anxiety about them.

Jesus invites us to let go of our worries—especially about our own inadequacy—and our unnecessarily high expectations with a surprising proposal. Jesus invites us to trade burdens with him: to give him our anxiety and harsh self-judgments, and to take on the burdens of *his* heart: gentleness and humility.

Something Jesus never doubted throughout his life was his Sonship—that he is God's Beloved One. Jesus took on our humanity and lived among us so that we could become just as sure that *we* are God's beloved. Gentleness begins with being compassionate with ourselves, seeing ourselves always in the light of God's love.

Humility is another word for truth. Jesus invites us to accept the truth about ourselves, as we truly are: our gifts, our goodness, our potential and our desires, as well as our limitations. Rather than fretting about our real limitations, we are invited to simply accept them. We can learn to work with them or around them, if we can accept ourselves for who we are.

This Gospel passage is more than an invitation: it is Jesus' promise that he will be with us at our most tired and vulnerable moments. We can take just a couple of quiet moments with Jesus now, handing over to him our fears and worries. We are not alone. Jesus is an understanding companion, inviting us to be accepting and gentle with ourselves, and sharing any burdens we carry.

Through the Day

Lord, refresh my spirit with the gentle reassurance that in you, I will be okay.

————◀◦▶————

23 I let go of needing perfect results, entrusting them to God.

"If it's not perfect, I've failed."

Anne has been an efficient perfectionist all her life: as a student, as a dancer, as a secretary. But now that she has several children, efficiency feels like a distant dream. Feeding, cleaning, and cuddling her little ones fills her days. She's never able to catch up with all that needs to be done in their small home. What about a thorough spring cleaning? Or preparing a special dinner or dessert? Unable to get anything done except caring for the children's immediate needs, Anne carries a haunting sense of failure.

One night, Anne's husband, Ron, comes home to find dinner late, the living room still cluttered with toys, and his wife discouraged. He asks her what's wrong. She sighs, "I've been working all day long and didn't get anything done!"

Ron looks over at the children happily playing. "You took care of our children all day. They're fed, they're clean, they're happy. What could be more important?" He leans over and kisses her. "Dinner on time is irrelevant."

Anne's heart lifts with this reminder of her *real* life's work—lovingly raising their children. The relentless perfectionism that had crushed her, preventing her from taking joy in her life, is banished.

From God's Heart to Yours

"Commit your way to the LORD; trust in him, and he will act" (Ps 37:5).

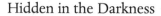

Hidden in the Darkness

The faith-filled perspective of Psalm 37 is just what we need when we feel perfectionism sneaking in or taking over. The psalmist invites us to entrust our "way" to God, because ultimately, God is in charge of our lives.

God makes many promises in the Scriptures, but never promises success or perfection. Perfectionism is a myth in which we pretend we are like God, that we can be or at least are supposed to be, perfect. Mistakes and human limitations do not fit into a perfectionist's plan.

Perfectionism narrows our vision to our own expectations and illusions. Those of us who are perfectionists try to control what is beyond control: outcomes, the future, and other people. Perfectionists ignore human limitations, and check off "to do" lists to give a sense of tangible security. But at its core, perfectionism is incompatible with faith—it's a trap, a fruitless searching for security in superficial realities that don't last.

Faith, instead, seeks to discover the big picture—God's perspective. Faith clings to God as the Almighty, as Creator and Provider, as Merciful Redeemer, as our Beginning and End, as the greatest Security we could ever have. Faith counts on the *intangible:* the promise and presence of the Spirit of Jesus who lovingly transforms our lives and the world.

God cares less about efficiency and results and more about intention and trust. God delights in surprising us, in bringing grace into ordinary, flawed situations. Teaching a child that she is loved, giving hope to a co-worker, listening to the concerns of a cancer-stricken friend—these may not be in our plan for the day, but they could be the fruit God wants us to bear.

When we let go of our perfectionism and our own expectations, we are free: free to live in the moments as God gives them to us. We can recognize and appreciate

God's quiet, faithful presence, and be ready to hear God's invitations.

Through the Day

Lord Jesus, I let go of my own expectations, and I trust in you working in me and through me.

———◄◦►———

24 I thank God for making me unique.

"At least I'm doing better than him/her."

Several months after beginning piano lessons with first grader Joanne, a piano teacher started lessons with her enthusiastic classmate Elizabeth. One day Joanne came to her lesson in tears. The two girls had begun to compare their progress on the way to school. Although Joanne had started her lessons earlier, Elizabeth was now ahead of her.

The piano teacher felt this competition between six-year-olds was unhealthy. At Elizabeth's next lesson, the piano teacher sternly told her that comparing her playing with Joanne's was wrong. It made Joanne feel bad. When Elizabeth solemnly nodded, the teacher thought that was the end of it.

But the next week, Elizabeth's mother called to cancel her lessons, saying, "She won't tell me why, but she does not want to come anymore. She's very upset."

Elizabeth's quickness to gloat over her speedy progress hid a deep insecurity that the teacher's reprimand set off. The unhealthy competition caused both girls to lose out: from then on, Joanne considered herself a slow learner, and Elizabeth gave up learning something she loved.

From God's Heart to Yours

"If we live by the Spirit, let us also be guided by the Spirit. Let us not become conceited, competing against one another, envying one another" (Gal 5:25–26).

Hidden in the Darkness

In the Letter to the Galatians, Saint Paul cautions us about competing with and comparing ourselves to another (cf. Gal 6:4 and 6:14). Restricted to its proper sphere, competition can be healthy and motivate us to excel. Making judgments and comparisons about our abilities and those of others is essential for working together and learning from one another.

But the spirit of competition can easily overflow into other areas of our life, which would be better served by a spirit of gratitude or service. When a competitive spirit takes over, we often judge people, instead of evaluating qualities or abilities. Judging others isn't helpful, because every person is a mystery. And comparing ourselves with others can lead us to feeling complacent, inadequate, or jealous. We might try to bolster our self-image by setting ourselves up as "better than." We forget that each person's uniqueness defies categories and comparisons.

Ultimately everything that we are and have, we receive as gift. Giftedness is key to our identity. We cannot take credit for our natural abilities, nor for the time or circumstances we've been given. Even our choices and efforts can be assisted by God's grace. This doesn't mean we put ourselves down, but that we recognize the fullness of our identity. Being gifted by God means that we are deeply loved. *We rejoice*, both in our giftedness and in the way we can use our gifts to shape ourselves, others, and the world around us.

A great attitude that can replace an overdeveloped sense of competition is to rejoice in others' gifts and learn from them whenever we can. Similarly, when we witness someone making a mistake or choosing poorly, we learn what not to do.

Comparing ourselves with someone else as "better" or "worse" flattens us and the other person into one dimension. We're so much more than any one gift or ability. Saint Paul reminds us that our true "boast" is in Jesus' saving love for us: "May I never boast of anything except the cross of our Lord Jesus Christ..." (Gal 6:14).

Through the Day

My Jesus, when I'm tempted to compete or compare myself with another, remind me that I am irreplaceable to you.

————◄◦►————

25 Silence invites me to remember God's loving kindness.

"I can't sit still; I have to be doing something."

Our noisy lives give us few opportunities to appreciate the benefits of silence. Silence can make us uncomfortable because, without external distractions, negative thoughts or unpleasant feelings can well up inside. At these times, silence can feel like torture.

Vietnamese priest and bishop Francis Xavier Nguyen Van Thuan appreciated silence and contemplation. After Van Thuan was named archbishop of Saigon, the Communist government imprisoned him from 1975 to 1989. Archbishop Van Thuan spent many years in the enforced silence of solitary confinement, but the first period—lasting eight months—was his darkest. Van Thuan's cruel imprisonment was designed to break him. After several months of unrelenting silence, Van Thuan felt hopelessness and uselessness overwhelm him. He became so weak and dispirited that he often couldn't pray, unable to even remember the words of the Our Father. Would he spend the rest of his life futilely abandoned in prison?

One day when he could pray, Van Thuan received a sudden insight: his relationship with God was more important than anything he could ever *do*. Even in prison, even if he forgot how to pray, he could continue to love God.

This insight, that God could still be first in his life, transformed the silence. From a prisoner of despair, Van Thuan became a witness to hope. He spent the rest of his imprisonment and the years after his release sharing the gift of hope he had received.

From God's Heart to Yours

"[H]e leads me beside still waters; he restores my soul"
(Ps 23:2–3).

Hidden in the Darkness

Silence can bring us to deeper prayer and self-awareness, but at times, we may find it easier to avoid silence than to rest in it. We might not realize that we're really running away from ourselves.

As Psalm 23 reminds us, silence can help us enter more deeply into the peace and refreshment God wants to give us. But sometimes in silence, the feelings we don't want to face—such as self-hate, fear that God is absent from our lives, or fear that we are unlovable—can completely take over. Then even the brief quiet of a daily morning offering can feel threatening. Silence no longer leads to an encounter with God, but to a door slammed shut.

When this happens, it's easy to give up on prayer altogether. But we need that time of connection with God to live fruitfully what we're going through. In Psalm 23, God's desire for us in the silence is that we are restored in the depths of our being. We can "take back" the silence by bringing God's Word into it.

Silence usually makes us more aware of our feelings and thoughts, which is important if we want to be fully present to our own lives. But our feelings need not overwhelm us. After honestly acknowledging them, the next step for us is to look at our feelings in the light of the Word of God. God's Word will challenge the faulty conclusions we often draw from our feelings. For example, we can replace the false conviction that we are unlovable with the truth that God lovingly leads us, even if we can't see him, hear him, or feel his presence.

The light of the Scriptures transforms how we perceive our experience and silence itself. No longer threatening, silence can once again help us pray and be refreshed by God's love for us.

Through the Day

God who speaks in the silence, I listen for your loving voice.

———◦———

26 My weaknesses can be entry ways for God's grace.

"I hate being weak!"

Last winter, I was extremely busy. When the urgency of what I was working on finally eased, I didn't take time to rest and reprioritize, but instead let myself get caught up in busy self-importance. I half realized that I'd fallen into the old trap of valuing myself only for my accomplishments, but I was too busy to stop myself. I caught something else, too—a cold. But the cold wouldn't leave; it kept getting worse. I finally went to the doctor, who diagnosed flu *and* a return of long-absent asthma. For several weeks, I was miserable: the antibiotics didn't seem to help; I couldn't lie down without coughing; and I would have given anything for one good night's sleep.

What added most to my physical discomfort was my feeling of being useless. Despite the other sisters' kindness and generosity with me, I couldn't shake the feeling that I was a burden, so every few days I decided I *must* be getting better and tried to go back to work. After almost two months of this, I finally gave up. I made a retreat over several days in bed. I was able to finally let go of my plans and goals, and entrust the future into Jesus' hands. During the retreat, I realized that Jesus was offering me a long-awaited grace: the gift to accept that I am loved for who I am rather than for what I accomplish. After this retreat, I finally started to recover.

Isn't it ironic that the very weakness I despised so much in myself—my illness and inability to work—became the way God gave me the grace I needed most?

From God's Heart to Yours

"My grace is sufficient for you, for power is made perfect in weakness" (2 Cor 12:9).

Hidden in the Darkness

These striking words from 2 Corinthians are actually Jesus' words to Saint Paul when he was praying that his "thorn in the flesh" would be taken away. We don't know what it was—a physical weakness? A personality flaw? The hardships of being an apostle? His concern for the way-wardness of one of the churches?

While we do not know what Paul's weakness was, we can sympathize. How many times have we prayed for God to free us from our vulnerability? Yet, when we accept them, weaknesses of any kind can give us new insight and perspective.

Our God who has no limitations seems to *rejoice* in working through the very limits and weaknesses we would cast aside. We usually call our weaknesses our "shadows," but it is in these very shadows that Jesus delights in shining the most brilliant light.

God seems to work more freely in us through our limitations. Is it because our weaknesses are the one area in our lives where we admit we aren't "in control," and so we allow God to come near to us and take over? If God can rejoice in working through our weaknesses, then we no longer need to let them bother us. We can simply accept our limitations for what they are and entrust them to God. Saint Paul puts it this way: "So, I will boast all the more gladly of my weaknesses, so that the power of Christ may dwell in me" (2 Cor 12:9).

Through the Day

My Jesus, I invite you in through the doorway of my weakness.

———◄○►———

27 God's mercy is greater than my sinfulness.

"I am too sinful for God to love me."

How do we grow in healthy self-esteem when we come face-to-face with our own sinfulness?

When Peter first encountered Jesus, he already knew himself well. Witnessing his first miracle, Peter pleaded his own unworthiness: "Go away from me, Lord, for I am a sinful man!" (Lk 5:8) But Jesus invited Peter to follow him, and Peter, trusting in Jesus, did follow him.

Fast forward to the night before Jesus' death. After Jesus was arrested, Peter tried to stay close to him. But when he was accused of being Jesus' companion, Peter, probably fearful of losing his life, denied knowing Jesus. Three times. The Gospel of Luke says, "The Lord turned and looked at Peter. And Peter … went out and wept bitterly" (22:61–62).

That night, Peter was forced to confront his own sinfulness. It must have been a truly horrible time of remorse and self-recrimination. Yet, surprisingly, this is not the last we hear of Peter. He is very much present in the Resurrection accounts, most noticeably by the lakeshore, when Jesus, acknowledging Peter's denials, asks Peter to confirm his love for him three times. How was Peter able to "recover" from such a sinful action? Why didn't he give up on himself?

From God's Heart to Yours

"[T]he LORD, my God, lights up my darkness" (Ps 18:28).

"Look to him, and be radiant; so your faces shall never be ashamed" (Ps 34:5).

Hidden in the Darkness

The truth about ourselves is multifaceted. We are loved by God. We are also free human persons, who have the ability to choose evil as well as good. Our sinfulness is a part of us for which we have to take responsibility; our neediness and weakness are as much a part of us as our giftedness.

But Psalm 18 reminds us that we are never alone, even in the darkness of our own sinfulness and guilt. If we were the center of our own lives, abandoned to ourselves, then sinfulness and remorse could easily overcome us. But we aren't alone.

God knows us better than we could ever know ourselves, and even knowing our sinfulness, God does not abandon us. God sent Jesus to help us to understand our human condition, and to lead us out of the darkness of sin into the light of God's grace.

Even when we sin, God has this amazing way of taking the worst things and bringing something good out of them. It's not that God wants evil to happen, but if we choose to do something wrong, then God can take even that and bring something good from it.

So, how could Peter turn so quickly from his denial of Jesus to a renewal of his commitment to Jesus, even with his self-doubts? Because Peter followed the advice of Psalm 34—he didn't keep the focus on himself. Peter had personally witnessed the new life that sprang from Jesus' encounters with sinners. He also must have remembered Jesus' parables of the prodigal son and the lost sheep. Peter's secret was this: even as he acknowledged his own sinfulness, he *focused* on the mercy and grace that God was offering him through Jesus. Even when Peter failed Jesus so terribly, he remembered Jesus' love for him.

"Look to him, and be radiant; so your faces shall never be ashamed."

Jesus invites us to do the same.

Through the Day

Jesus, I immerse my weakness and shame in the ocean of your love and mercy.

———◂◉▸———

28 God gives me feelings to enrich my life and shape my actions.

"I feel guilty when I am angry/sad/envious or _____."

When I was a child, I thought good people never got angry, never wanted what they couldn't have, never felt sadness or envy. I thought I must be very bad because I had not just some, but *all* of those feelings.

Many people are uncomfortable with acknowledging or displaying the feelings that our culture interprets as negative—feelings such as anger, sadness, envy, and guilt. But feelings are fundamentally neutral—they are simple and unwilled reactions to our perception of a situation. It is only in expressing or acting on them without concern for others that they can be negative or harmful.

Jesus seemed quite at home with the full range of his feelings and used them freely to communicate. Jesus delighted in using paradox in his parables to shock people out of their assumptions and into thinking for themselves. In the Gospels, Jesus is by turns gentle, witty, direct, humorous, probing, challenging, and wise.

By taking on our humanness, Jesus sanctified it—even the so-called negative feelings. Yet deep down, many of us are still ashamed of having these feelings. What is important is not what feelings we have, but what we choose to do with them.

From God's Heart to Yours

"In the temple he [Jesus] found people selling cattle, sheep, and doves, and the money-changers seated at their tables. Making a whip of cords, he drove all of them out of the temple, both the sheep and the cattle.... He told those who were selling the doves, 'Take those things out of here! Stop making my Father's house a marketplace!'"(Jn 2:14–16)

Hidden in the Darkness

This Gospel passage gives us an image of Jesus with which we may not be fully comfortable. But Jesus teaches us not only with his words, but also by his example.

Unfortunately, in a world marked by sinfulness and injustice, anger is often a fitting response. Jesus used his justifiable anger to deliberately and dramatically end the dishonoring of God's house. Yet his anger was not out of proportion or destructive. Jesus stopped the offensive behavior, but without hurting others. His dramatic actions taught a memorable lesson about the sanctity of the Father. He spoke convincingly (if mysteriously) to the temple officials who challenged him. Jesus used his feelings in accord with God's purpose for them: as indicators of his perceptions of a situation.

Feelings can tell us a lot about ourselves and the way we perceive the world. Feelings also add richness to our experience and to our responses to others. Compassion is born of our own hurt. Anger can give us the extra passion or strength that we need to stand against injustice. We can express our feelings within a context of seeking to build love and respect as Jesus did. We allow our feelings to inform our choices, but not to dictate them.

Jesus' example can help us to navigate the muddy waters of the feelings *we* find difficult to handle. By acknowledging that what we feel is important, we build our personal integrity. When we take the next step and use our reason, conscience, intuition, and experience to shape the way we respond to the situation that has evoked such strong feelings in us, we contribute our unique voice and perspective to the world.

Through the Day

Jesus, Son of God and Son of Mary, sanctify my feelings and how I choose to express them today.

———◦———

29 God invites me to walk through fear into trust.

"I am ashamed of being such a coward!"

It was a new retail clerk's nightmare, and it happened on Amy's second day. She was standing behind the counter when a man with nervous eyes walked in, pointed the pocket of his dirty tan coat at her, and demanded the money from the register.

Training hadn't covered this. Did the guy have a gun? She didn't want to risk anyone getting hurt—not herself, and especially not the elderly staff person working in the back. Amy opened the drawer and began pulling out bills—everything except the alarmed $20 bill. She hoped he wouldn't notice; Amy didn't know whether the alarm was silent. The man waved his pocket/gun at the bill she'd skipped. "Hurry up! Everything!" Heart pounding, she looked up. "Coins, too?" The thief grinned. "No, but I do want *that*." Time froze. Amy tugged at the alarmed $20, and it came free—silently! The thief grabbed the money and ran out of the store.

While waiting for the police to arrive, another clerk told Amy, "He's tried it before. He doesn't really have a gun. Last time we just told him to get out!"

Amy's throat tightened. Perhaps the clerk meant to comfort her, but she had done the opposite. Now Amy had a double burden: not just the terror of the experience, but the shame of having been tricked into showing fear.

From God's Heart to Yours

"Do not fear, for I have redeemed you; I have called you by name, you are mine" (Isa 43:1).

Hidden in the Darkness

Throughout the Bible, one phrase repeats over and over again, like a chant: *Do not fear.* God knows we need to hear him reassure us many times, especially when, like Amy, we become ashamed of our fear or start to feel trapped in it.

We never need to feel ashamed of being afraid. If our fear becomes overwhelming, we may need to confront our fears, or work with anxiety-reducing techniques. But we can also learn from our fear. Fear shows us what is important to us, what we are afraid to lose. Fear reminds us of our powerlessness.

Our frailty and vulnerability are part of why our lives are so precious. Yet, many of us go through life not paying attention to what is most important. We are conditioned by our daily routine, comforts, and conveniences into thinking that we are in control of our lives. Fear shocks us into remembering the truth that we aren't in control. But the refrain of God's Word reminds of a deeper truth: even if *we* do not have control over own lives, God does. *Do not fear.*

When we remain in our comfort zone, we become blind to the miracles of every day. God can use the discomfort of our fear as an invitation, a doorway through which he can lead us to a new understanding of and trust in his providence. Being s-c-a-r-e-d can lead us to recognize the S-A-C-R-E-D in our lives.

When we leave routine behind and choose to live in the grace and miracle of the present moment, we quickly realize how our life is unspeakably frail, unutterably precious, and unimaginably tended by God. We can grab hold of the amazing opportunities we are given. We can live in the security of utter reliance on God.

Through the Day

Jesus, when I am scared, let me rediscover the sacred in my life.

---

30 Loneliness puts me in touch with my need to connect.

"I hate feeling lonely!"

Michael went with his young adult group to a weekend retreat because his friends pressured him, even though he was sure he would be bored. Friday evening, Michael was horrified to discover that it was to be a silent retreat. The retreatants were not to talk to one another, and they were encouraged to "unplug"—no cell phones, no music, and no Internet.

Michael's heart sank. He *knew* he shouldn't have come. As the evening wore on, Michael's restlessness grew. He realized that he wasn't just bored, but lonely. "This is silly," he reasoned with himself. "I can handle a little quiet time."

When Michael woke Saturday morning, he decided to go hiking through the woods. As he trekked, Michael pondered his experience from the night before. "Why did I feel so lonely?" he worried. "I have my friends and family." But as he looked around the woods, a sense of loneliness swept through him again.

Later, the retreat director reassured Michael that his experience was normal and might be an invitation. "Ask the Lord to show you what you are missing in your life," the director encouraged. "God might be leading you."

Many of us think that if we feel lonely something is wrong with us. Our culture encourages this view, saturating us with information and noise that block our awareness of feelings of emptiness.

From God's Heart to Yours

"I will now allure her, and bring her into the wilderness, and speak tenderly to her" (Hos 2:14).

Hidden in the Darkness

In the Scriptures, going off into the wilderness or desert to be radically "alone with God" was considered a difficult but privileged and sacred time.

Being alone or away from our loved ones can trigger feelings of loneliness. But sometimes we can be loneliest in the midst of a crowd. Loneliness is often about feeling disconnected—from God, ourselves, and others. As uncomfortable as loneliness is, it can also contain an invitation.

When we feel lonely, the first step simply might be to accept our experience for what it is—part of being human. Loneliness has nothing to do with what we deserve, or whether we are "worthy" of friends. We don't need to feel bad or down on ourselves for being lonely.

Secondly, we can recognize in our loneliness our need for love and for a deeper connection with others—and decide to do something about it. Loneliness can increase our appreciation for the healthy relationships we do have, and encourage us to grow in those relationships. Loneliness can push us to reach out to old friends and to seek new ones.

Finally, feelings of loneliness can prompt us to enter into the wilderness of our own hearts so we can reconnect with ourselves and the Lord. Spending time alone or "in the wilderness" may allow us to become aware of our hidden feelings and desires. When we are more self-aware, we enter more easily into a deeper encounter with God.

Our relationship with God and our relationship with ourselves are foundational for the rest of our lives. And yet, we are often "too busy" to take the time to nurture these relationships. Loneliness can be the reminder we need to take time for these foundational relationships: to reconnect with God and his tremendous love for us, and to remember to value our own thoughts, feelings, and experiences.

Through the Day

Lord, today I will take a quiet moment to reconnect with you and with myself.

———◦———

31 I can use criticism as an invitation to learn.

"Criticism makes me feel really down."

Margaret wrote her first story when she was seven. But when she tried to read it to her father, he fell asleep. After she won an essay contest in grade seven, her teacher told her that another student—her best friend—deserved the prize more. At college, the professor of her first (and last) writing class called her essay "conventional and trivial." Margaret decided to give up writing.

Recently, however, as part of a class, Margaret was asked to compose her own "writing autobiography." As she did so, the perspective of time helped her discover that much of the criticism she'd received had little to do with her writing ability. But because she hadn't really examined it at the time, she'd allowed the criticism to block her from taking her writing seriously.

Margaret has since decided to forgive those who criticized her, and is happily pursuing her dream of writing.

From God's Heart to Yours

"Those who ignore instruction despise themselves, but those who heed admonition gain understanding" (Prov 15:32).

"[T]he Lord disciplines those whom he loves" (Heb 12:6).

Hidden in the Darkness

If God loves us for who we are, we have no reason to feel ashamed when we are criticized. Many of us suffer from a tendency to make criticism a bigger deal than necessary. Constructive criticism is feedback about one action or attitude, *not* a reaction to who we are as a person. Seen in this way, criticism doesn't have to be devastating or overwhelming.

Our trust in God's love can help us take a step back from the criticism we receive in order to listen to it honestly, but discerningly. We can distinguish between constructive criticism that invites us to grow, and harmful criticism that discourages us.

When we listen carefully, we notice whether the critical remark is about a specific action or choice that we made, or about a particular aspect of ourselves. Then we can ask ourselves: Is there some truth in what the person said about my particular choice or about the circumstance? Perhaps God is using this person's words to invite me to change or to grow in a particular way. If we find truth in the evaluation, we can decide to adjust our behavior, or keep it in mind for the future. If we disagree, we simply let it go.

When the criticism is general, we have other options. If we sense the person is trying to be helpful, we can ask for more specifics. If, however, the person seems hostile, then we can either dismiss the comment or switch the focus to what the remark can tell us about the person or our relationship with him or her. Perhaps she is criticizing us in an effort to feel better about herself. Perhaps his expectations are too high. Perhaps she is simply having a bad day. In such cases, the criticism is about the other person, and not about us at all.

Regardless of what was said, when we are criticized and start to feel overwhelmed, we can remember that nothing anyone says has the power to change our value in God's eyes. Then we will have the inner balance to evaluate the critical remark honestly for what it is worth.

Through the Day

Jesus Master, teach me to discern your invitations so that I can become more like you.

———◦———

32 I acknowledge my dependence on God and others.

"I don't want to bother anybody."

Mira was one of the most vibrant teenagers I knew in high school. Strong, gifted, and high-spirited, she set out after graduation on an adventurous career path while staying in touch with her loving family. Although she seems to have everything, Mira hides a struggle with depression and anxiety that recently forced her to stop working.

By hiding her depression from the people who love her most, Mira has cut herself off from support—maybe from the very support she needs the most. She refuses any encouragement to visit a therapist. Perhaps she is convinced that she should be able to overcome this "on her own," or she is afraid to burden anyone else with her problems. Perhaps she is simply too ashamed to reveal her inner struggles to anyone else. Maybe "I don't want to bother anybody" really means "*I'm* not worth the bother to anyone." Many of us, like Mira, have a hard time admitting that we need or deserve help.

From God's Heart to Yours

"Our soul waits for the LORD; he is our help and shield. / Our heart is glad in him, because we trust in his holy name. / Let your steadfast love, O LORD, be upon us, even as we hope in you" (Ps 33:20–22).

Hidden in the Darkness

The psalms freely acknowledge our need for God. Despite the pressures of today's culture, none of us was created to be self-sufficient. There is no shame in our human neediness. Yet it can be hard to acknowledge our dependence on God. Sometimes it's even harder asking for help because we are convinced we don't deserve it.

One of the beauties of the psalms is their trusting acknowledgement of our need for God, the constant reaching out to God for help in every kind of difficulty. The images that Psalm 33 gives us, or hints at, are particularly striking: God's fidelity is a shield protecting us no matter what life throws at us. God cloaks us in love. God's love is our heart's gladness.

The psalmist seems completely comfortable with the full spectrum of needs that comes with being human. He is sure God always hears our prayer and responds, even if it is in ways that are unexpected. To fully accept who we are as human beings, we too need to become comfortable with our dependence on God and on others, which includes admitting when we need help. There can be great relief in finally letting go of the lie that we have to do it all on our own.

As we acknowledge how much we need God, we can use the honest, grounded language of the psalms as a reminder that we can be absolutely fearless in telling God what we need. As we allow God's love to fill us, we can also ask for the wisdom to discern who God has placed in our lives to help us.

God gives us one another to help us on our journey. God wants us to care for one another, to be the face of Christ for one another. In God's plan, no one is completely independent or dependent; we are all interdependent.

Through the Day

Compassionate Lord, teach me to ask for help when I need it, and to offer help when I see another's need.

————◦————

33 From within the pain of loss, I can treasure the gift I have received.

"God has abandoned me."

Armina had a very special relationship with her father. When he died suddenly of a heart attack, Armina's grief was compounded. Not only had she lost her beloved father, she had not been able to tell him goodbye or how much she loved him.

Armina was staggered by the pain of her loss and the feeling that God had abandoned her. She took time off from work, spent extra time with her family, even escaped for a quiet week at the ocean. But she still couldn't sleep through the night, couldn't regain a sense of peace. The only thing that helped was running. She did a lot of that.

After crying through Christmas, she decided to go on a weekend retreat. Praying alone in the small chapel, she finally opened up to God. She began to tell Jesus why she needed her father so much, about everything for which she missed him. Suddenly she stopped. What a tremendous gift he had been! The time and love her father had shared with her, she would always have.

Armina spent the rest of the retreat thanking God for the gift of her father. The next months were not easy, but by focusing on the gift her father had been for her, Armina could finally begin to heal her grief.

From God's Heart to Yours

"I will go before you and level the mountains. . . . I will give you the treasures of darkness" (Isa 45:2–3).

Hidden in the Darkness

When we are devastated by loss and buried under a mountain of grief, we too can feel that God has abandoned us. Even Jesus, when he was on the cross, felt the absence of his Father. But no matter what we are feeling, we can count, as Jesus did, on God's faithful love for us. The Book of Isaiah, which contains some of the most consoling passages in the Bible, reminds us that God is with us even in the darkest moments.

Initially when we grieve the loss of someone we love, or something important to us, we can feel only the pain. Each of us experiences and expresses grief uniquely. Loss often brings us more into touch with our own neediness. We may feel ashamed of our inability to "recover quickly" from our grief. We might simply feel ashamed of feeling so bereft.

Great pain means great loss. And our loss is great only when the gift we were given was great. The memory of that gift can become a treasure upon which we build the rest of our lives. Our recognition of God's tenderness in giving us that gift can deepen our relationship with God and eventually our trust that God could never abandon us.

Even though we may no longer enjoy the gift of our loved one's presence, or that ability or opportunity we now miss in our life, our gratitude can help us to appreciate the other gifts in our lives that we often take for granted. The people who love us, the gifts of health and time— these are gifts that we can always appreciate more. After a time, even grief itself can be a gift that forms us to live in grateful awareness of our blessings.

Through the Day

Crucified Lord Jesus, broken on the cross, be with me in my brokenness.

———◦———

34 I look for the beauty of God's presence in the world.

"All I can see today is the shadow side of life."

I vividly remember my first few months in Manhattan: my head was perpetually craned upward. I just couldn't get over the novelty of skyscrapers towering above me or the surrealistic idea that I actually *lived* in the great city of New York. I really didn't care how silly I looked tripping over the cracks in the sidewalk. The new sights, sounds, and smells made the city crackle with life. I have since discovered that every city possesses its own unique beauty and begs for similar attention.

Once I accompanied a couple visiting Chicago for the first time. They refused to look up because others might think they were tourists. Later, all they remembered of the city were the shadows of the skyscrapers, the graffiti, the burned-out slums, the mind-numbing gray of endless concrete blocks. How much they missed!

Sometimes in our daily living, we don't look up to catch the view. Keeping our inner gaze fixed downward prevents us from seeing the daily beauty of our lives, the many ways God reveals his love for us.

From God's Heart to Yours

"May the Lord direct your hearts to the love of God and to the steadfastness of Christ" (2 Thes 3:5).

Hidden in the Darkness

In this passage from the Second Letter to the Thessalonians, Saint Paul reminds us of how important it is to focus on God's love and Christ's faithfulness. Paul is speaking about much more than the current self-help trend toward "positive thinking" that claims we can magically think through the obstacles of life in much the same way that Superman flies over tall buildings. An increasing number of self-help books assert that just repeating positive statements about ourselves or our future will change our lives in that direction. These claims deny the harsh realities of life, as well as each person's free will, and reduce positive thinking to mere superstition.

Positive thinking can be a helpful attitude adjustment that enables us to clarify and enrich our perceptions of ourselves and the world around us. But positive thinking still keeps the focus on us and our own agenda. Paul, instead, prays for something quite different: that we will shift our focus away from ourselves and onto God's saving love for us in Christ.

Centering our lives on the simple reality that God loves us *no matter what* is a life-changing shift in perception. We shed the illusions and false assumptions we've carried and begin to glimpse the deeper meaning and beauty in our lives.

Focusing on God's love for us opens us up to discover the true landscape of our life, our lifescape. By keeping our gaze focused downward, on ourselves, or on the difficult areas of our life, we exclude Christ from our line of sight, just as new visitors to the city miss the skyline by not looking up. Directing our inner gaze toward God, we discover how the beauty of Christ's presence fills our lives.

Paul invites us to direct not just our thoughts but our entire being toward God's love and Christ's fidelity. Centered on Jesus, we can welcome God's grace more fully, open ourselves to his presence in others, and make decisions that are more loving and life-giving. We can be completely transformed by God's love for us in Christ.

Through the Day

Open my eyes, Lord, to the saving beauty of your love for me.

————◄○►————

35 I cling to God's steadfastness in times of change.

"I don't like change."

Corazon lived through her first earthquake when she traveled to a conference in the West. In her room on the twenty-fourth floor of a hotel, she was suddenly awakened in the middle of the night. The floor was shaking and her bed was jumping up and down.

"It was the weirdest feeling," she told friends later. "I'm used to hurricanes, high winds, hail, and floods. But

I couldn't get used to the ground *shaking*." The earthquake was over quickly and didn't cause any serious damage. But Corazon couldn't get back to sleep that night, and didn't sleep well until she returned home to the East Coast.

We have all experienced those big transitions that shake the ground of our life: a shift in an important relationship, moving to a new city or new home, getting a new job or leaving an old one.

Life is *full* of unsettling changes—big and small. How can we respond to transition or change in a way that helps us to grow instead of stressing us out?

From God's Heart to Yours

"Our steps are made firm by the LORD, when he delights in our way; / though we stumble, we shall not fall headlong, / for the LORD holds us by the hand" (Ps 37:23–24).

Hidden in the Darkness

The steadiness of our path is often a subjective perception. We may feel comfortable in the way we're going, when God can see it's leading us to a precipice. Although many of the psalms invite us to walk in the way of the Lord, Psalm 37 reminds us that it is not the path we should rely on, but the Lord himself, who steadies us with his loving guidance no matter how unsteady or potholed our path may be. Even when we trip in unfamiliar surroundings, God catches us.

Walking steadily down an uneven path is a good image for negotiating our way through change. While change is unsettling, it can have hidden benefits. For one, the discomfort change brings is a reminder that our hearts are made for the Unchangeable One. Nothing less than the eternal God can satisfy the deepest longings of our hearts. God's rocklike fidelity is the security to which we cling when everything around us seems unreliable.

Change has another unexpected benefit: it can be an opportunity to deepen our trust in God, to experience how God holds us by the hand. Because the uncertainty of change or transition can make us feel as if our life is slipping out of control, we often seek to exercise control over another aspect of our life—maybe by cleaning, reorganizing, or undertaking a physical workout. (If you have ever regained a sense of peace after energetically cleaning the kitchen, you'll know what I mean.)

Transition reminds us not to take things for granted. We are not in control of everything. Psalm 37 grounds us in the truth that God is not just our emergency Rescuer, but is truly in charge of our lives. God may use the very situations we want to avoid—like unplanned detours—to invite us to something new.

In our anxiety, we may not feel a sense of God's presence, but we can be sure that God will keep his promise to be with us always.

Through the Day

Jesus, I lean on the rock of your faithful love for me.

———◦——

36   I invite Jesus to teach me to be gentle.

"Why can't I get this right?"

Mary learned to knit as a youngster but never went back to it until her children had grown. She joined a knitting class and quickly became a vital member, hosting it in her own home. After only a couple of projects, Mary began picking the prettiest patterns even if they were somewhat intricate, and the results were exquisite. Yet Mary's impossibly high expectations were never completely satisfied, no matter how beautiful her handiwork turned out.

Gradually, the class developed into a knitting circle, called "The Knit-Wits." As the members became better acquainted, Mary became known as "the unraveler" because she would unravel her work at the tiniest imperfection. Over time, the circle's gentle acceptance and her own increasing proficiency have helped Mary realize that "handmade" includes the unevenness and endearing quirks that make each knitted item unique.

She still enjoys the challenge of knitting an item as perfectly as possible, but her daughters, who used to believe their mother's self-deprecating comments, now beg her for hand-knit sweaters and baby blankets.

High standards encourage us to fulfill our potential. But being too hard on ourselves not only prevents us from taking joy in our accomplishments but also can limit or sabotage our power to make a difference in the lives of others.

From God's Heart to Yours

"[L]et your adornment be the inner self with the lasting beauty of a gentle and quiet spirit, which is very precious in God's sight" (1 Pet 3:4).

Hidden in the Darkness

This passage from the First Letter of Peter, set within the context of living as a servant of God in suffering, specifically addresses how wives can win over their husbands by their good example. But it also works as a wonderful starting point in any relationship—beginning with how we relate to ourselves.

Described here as a spiritual jewel cherished by God, gentleness is usually considered a personality trait, not a virtue. But Jesus himself invites us to model ourselves on his gentleness (cf. Mt 11:29). As Messiah, Jesus was surrounded by great expectations, yet despite others' rejection and the apparent failure of his mission, Jesus never blamed himself. Jesus also never imposed himself on others. His relationships with others were characterized by openness and invitation, traits of gentleness.

Harshness, the opposite of gentleness, is a singularly dark view of life and does a kind of violence to the spirit by imposing only one view—its own judgment. Because it always assumes the worst, harshness rarely allows us to see the truth.

Gentleness is a nonviolent approach to life that does not impose itself on others. Yet, it is not weakness. It requires deep strength to seek respectfully to resolve conflict without resorting to violence—even the common everyday violence with which we try to manipulate others, such as a harsh tone of voice, passive-aggressive behavior, or blaming. Gentleness detaches us from one way of looking at things—right or wrong, black or white—and allows us to relate respectfully to both ourselves and others.

The First Letter of Peter fittingly pairs gentleness with quietness: being quiet allows us to hear; being gentle allows us to take in what we hear.

Because gentleness and harshness are both attitudes that easily become habitual, we need to practice gentleness with ourselves as well as with others. Being gentle with ourselves will lead us to treat both ourselves and others more kindly—the way Jesus relates to us.

Through the Day

Jesus Master, teach me your way of gentleness.

37 I entrust what is beyond my control to God.

"Why can't anyone else do anything right?"

Linda is an independent television producer with extraordinary talent who consistently produces beautiful work. Actual production is demanding, requiring both immense preparation and spontaneous improvisation. At any moment, dozens of things—many beyond her control—can go wrong. At these intense and occasionally chaotic moments, Linda's artistic expectations do not always serve her well. She doesn't realize that during production, her natural tendencies are heightened: her perfectionism can become finicky and impossible to please; her insights can be barbed; and her sensitivity can develop into excessive mood swings.

Over time, some of her collaborators have become hesitant to work with her again. High expectations and the tension of creatively coping with the unexpected drive Linda into extremely controlling behavior. She is starting to realize that, if she wants to continue to work collaboratively, she has to stop being so controlling.

Needing a sense of control about our lives is healthy and important. Yet, what do we actually have control over? *Only our own choices and actions.*

We are often unrealistic and expect to control what is beyond us. All of us experience moments of panic when we realize that something we value is slipping out of our control. This is when we feel our powerlessness most acutely, and it can push us into a frantic panic that irrationally tries to control the uncontrollable.

From God's Heart to Yours

"[A]part from me you can do nothing" (Jn 15:5).

Hidden in the Darkness

Jesus reminds us that the ultimate outcome of our lives is not in our control, but in his. This is a huge comfort when we bump up against our own limitations. While it can be terrifying to admit how limited, vulnerable, and powerless we are, our powerlessness is only a small part of the picture. Jesus doesn't say: "Apart from me you can do some things." Jesus reminds us that *everything* we seek to do, everything about our lives, is ultimately in God's hands. We are continually sustained by our loving God.

When we stand beneath a mountain, gaze at a breathtaking sunset, or look up in awe at the night sky full of stars, we feel our littleness. Yet we can also feel cherished: we have been given these majestic mountains, this glowing sunset, those sparkling stars. What a relief and joy it is to believe that the omnipotent God has our best interests at heart!

What if we were not responsible for making that event go perfectly, or for the traffic that made us late, or the unexpected glitch, or the imperfect behavior of a co-worker? What if we didn't need to control the unexpected? Our humanity and limitations are part of God's plan for us. When we try to control the uncontrollable, we are disrespectful of others, ourselves, and God's plan.

Accepting our limits and working within them is responding to God's plan. Suddenly, instead of working with jaw clenched, always looking over our shoulder, we can focus on our own choices and actions, and begin to trust that God will work with and through whatever life brings.

When we discover and accept our unique place in the plan of God, we find unimaginable freedom. Jesus offers us that freedom today.

Through the Day

Lord, I am yours. Everything else I entrust to your loving wisdom.

———◀◦▶———

PART 3

GOD'S BELOVED
IN THE WORLD

38 I live in touch with my own truth wherever I am.

"Who I am depends on who I am with."

Karen prides herself on her stylish appearance. She is forever trying to lose weight, although she doesn't need to. She wears clothes that are considered "in" instead of what she likes. Karen tries really hard to please her friends and co-workers. Even her conversations are usually about what is going on in others' lives, not about her. Recently, however, she has started to feel that no one really knows her. "I feel like who I am is getting a bit lost," she says. "I think I might be adapting too much, hiding behind their expectations and needs. I'm not sure I even know how to be myself with them."

Many people find themselves in a similar dilemma. The media pressure women to look and act in a certain way. Each situation and group of people we belong to seems to have different expectations. We put on and take off various identities throughout the day. Caught up in others' expectations, we can lose track of our deeper identity.

Perhaps the underlying fear is that if we are truly ourselves, our co-workers or friends might reject us. But if we never reveal our deeper selves to others, we run the risks of loneliness, of being misunderstood, of living superficially, or of compromising our own integrity.

From God's Heart to Yours

"God is true" (Jn 3:33).

Hidden in the Darkness

God is absolutely and eternally true—faithful to himself and to us. God blesses each of us with unique identities and gifts that he wants us to share with the world. If we deny or leave out vital aspects of ourselves in our close relationships, we cannot be the blessing God intends us to be. God calls us to be ourselves in the world.

We frequently must adapt to various relationships and circumstances. While adapting may require giving up something we want or even need, it never means that we leave behind who we are. But when our identity is fragile or our self-esteem is low, we can blur the boundaries. We can adapt too much to accommodate a particular person. Imprisoned by the fear of what others will think of us, we are afraid to express our own needs, concerns, or opinions. Lack of communication leads to misunderstanding, resentment, conflict, lack of closeness, dominance of one person's needs or opinions over those of the other, and similar outcomes. We cannot make a gift of ourselves if we have forgotten or left behind who we are.

The strength of any relationship is founded on the respect each person has for the other. In healthy relationships, people learn how to respond to one another's needs while at the same time maintaining their own identity and taking care of their own concerns.

Healthy boundaries help us to respect each person's God-given individuality and freedom and enable us to avoid being enmeshed in another's feelings or responsibilities. Healthy boundaries provide space and respect, strengthening our individual identities. Each of us is free to speak and act from the core of our identity, rather than from a false sense of guilt, obligation, or entanglement.

We are called to make a gift of ourselves to others—a gift that only we can give. The freer we are, the more fully we can engage in authentic relationships with others.

Through the Day

Lord, help me to be the gift to others that you created me to be!

---

39 I accept both my giftedness and weakness, secure in God's love.

"If only I had done more."

The film *Amazing Grace* is the true story of William Wilberforce, who, in the eighteenth century, undertook the enormous struggle of ending the slave trade in Great Britain. Wilberforce rediscovered his faith in God just as his political career was taking off. His close friend, soon-to-be Prime Minister William Pitt, challenged him to serve God through his political efforts.

Ahead of his time in recognizing the horrors and immorality of slavery, Wilberforce sacrificed his youth and health to this cause unsuccessfully for nineteen years. When the film starts, Wilberforce has been persuaded by concerned friends to give up the struggle in Parliament for the sake of his health. Midway through the film, Wilberforce, haunted by the faces of his brothers and sisters trapped in slavery, realizes that he simply cannot give up.

Wilberforce's passionate dedication to those who are enslaved becomes both his greatest strength *and* his greatest weakness: ultimately, his perseverance ends the slave trade; but because he cares so much, it also makes him vulnerable to others' attacks and costs him his health.

When we are fully living our true calling from God by responding wholeheartedly to the genuine needs of others, it can be difficult to harmonize the greatness of this calling with our very real limitations.

From God's Heart to Yours

"But we have this treasure in clay jars, so that it may be made clear that this extraordinary power belongs to God and does not come from us.... For while we live, we are always being given up to death for Jesus' sake, so that the life of Jesus may be made visible" (2 Cor. 4:7, 11).

Hidden in the Darkness

Saint Paul's image of the treasure held in a fragile clay jar perfectly captures the paradox of our life in Christ: the immensity of our call and our littleness in the face of it. This wonderful image is one key to understanding the essential virtue of humility.

Christian literature from earlier times is sometimes misunderstood as promoting a humility that is at odds with healthy self-esteem. But humility is actually a foundation for self-esteem because humility is a clear recognition of the truth about us and God.

We are frail human beings, liable to crash and shatter in an instant. Yet our fragility is astoundingly blessed with God's graced invitations. Humility is the virtue that enables us to dare to accept both our fragility and the splendid treasures with which God gifts us.

A faith-filled friend once shared this image with me: each of us is like an hourglass. At the top of the hourglass is the wealth of grace that the Trinity pours out on us; the narrow neck through which that abundance squeezes is us, with our limits and weaknesses. As it passes through us, the sand expands into abundance for those people waiting for God's touch in their lives.

Because our identity is uniquely shaped by our gifts and limits, God lovingly invites each of us to participate in the divine plan of salvation in ways that are precisely suited to us. Humility helps us to accept fully our fragility and our giftedness, as well as their consequences—such as the likelihood that our fragile clayness will suffer from being so closely united to the weight of the precious treasure of our gifts. But even in that suffering, we can trust in God's loving plan for us.

Through the Day

Lord, I dedicate my fragile giftedness to serve you.

———◦———

40 In sufferings, I can count on God's special closeness to me.

"It's God's fault!"

How often, when something goes wrong, our reaction is to blame God.

An elderly woman shivers in an unheated apartment in subzero weather.

A child huddles in a corner after her father rapes her.

An alcoholic mother destroys her family's peace.

An innocent infant is stricken with a brain tumor.

An earthquake kills thousands of people.

War. The AIDS epidemic. Genocide. Terrorist attacks. Hate crimes. Child soldiers. Racism. Abortion. Euthanasia.

Sometimes our sufferings can be the consequence of bad choices made by us or by someone else. In these cases, the suffering may be an incentive to choose better the next time. But what about senseless suffering: illness, natural disaster, the suffering of the innocent caused by the ill will of others? How could God permit these to happen? Can God truly be all-powerful and all-good and allow these to happen? Has God abandoned us?

There are no easy answers, but the Word of God reassures us in one way: No one is ever abandoned in suffering. God, who sees everything, is mysteriously present, weeping beside us.

From God's Heart to Yours

"The LORD is near to the brokenhearted, and saves the crushed in spirit" (Ps 34:18).

"As [Jesus] came near and saw the city, he wept over it" (Lk 19:41).

Hidden in the Darkness

The mystery of suffering is the biggest challenge we face in living out our faith. Even Jesus did not attempt to explain the mystery of suffering—perhaps because it is a mystery beyond human comprehension or expression. Faith doesn't take away the mystery or the suffering, but offers us another mystery: that our God does not run from those who suffer, but instead draws close to them.

As people of faith called to love one another, we are responsible to try to prevent and alleviate the sufferings of others. When we can't, when the scope of a tragedy—in its breadth or depth or both—is untouched by our greatest efforts and abilities, then we seek answers. Like a child, we need to know why. Blaming God can be an easy out.

Psalm 34 offers us an extraordinary expression of faith: that God is particularly *near* to the brokenhearted; that God pays special attention to those devastated by suffering; *that God is with us in a special way when we suffer.*

When we are confronted with another's suffering that we cannot alleviate, our tendency is to run away. God, however, does the opposite. God draws close. Psalm 56 even talks about God collecting our tears and counting them one by one. Who is this tender God who doesn't run from our suffering, but instead draws closer to us?

If God wanted no part in our suffering, the Father would never have sent us his Son, Jesus. In Jesus, God draws especially close to our suffering. Jesus' life was full of hardships. He also had a predilection for those who suffered: the miracles Jesus performed most frequently were healings. Jesus himself fully lived the songs of the "suffering servant" found in the Book of Isaiah, bringing us salvation not only through his life and resurrection, but also through his horrifically painful sufferings and death.

The greatest tragedy—Jesus' death on the cross—mysteriously became God's greatest work. Somehow, in all of our sufferings, we too can mysteriously experience the fidelity of God. We entrust the sufferings of the world to God's breaking heart.

Through the Day

Lord, I trust that you will never abandon me.

——◄○►——

41 God cares about my intentions and efforts, not whether I succeed.

"I feel like such a failure."

Would you attribute these words to a saint? From his letters and his superior's testimony, we know this was the sentiment of an unusual North American martyr, the Jesuit Saint Nöel Chabanel.

In 1643, Nöel was sent from his native France as a missionary to the native peoples of Canada. When he arrived, however, he found it impossible to adjust to life among the Hurons. The different standards of privacy, cleanliness and food, and overall living conditions repulsed him. Nöel had been a teacher in France, but here he couldn't even learn the Huron language. Like the other Jesuits, he faced the constant danger of death. Worst of all, Nöel became tormented by the thought he was a failure.

Nöel daily faced the temptation to give up and return home, where his efforts and talents could be appreciated. After four years of soul-searching and discernment, Nöel made an unprecedented act of trust in God. He vowed to remain in the Huron mission until he had given his life. Two years later, Nöel was martyred.

Other North American martyrs experienced great satisfaction in their efforts to proclaim Jesus. But Nöel had to face the realization that almost all of his efforts failed.

Feeling like a failure is a devastating experience that can shake us to the core. But failure can also be an unparalleled opportunity to grow in holiness, as it was for Nöel Chabanel.

From God's Heart to Yours

"Will the LORD spurn for ever, and never again be favorable? . . . I will meditate on all your work, and muse on your mighty deeds. / Your way, O God, is holy" (Ps 77:7, 12–13).

Hidden in the Darkness

For a moment, the psalmist seems to buy in to the false assumption that when we fail, it is because the Lord has rejected or spurned us. While it can certainly feel that way, the truth is that we often judge the results of our efforts by our own limited standards. God defines "success" and "failure" very differently. We forget that God has a bigger plan that includes our desires and choices but goes far beyond our comprehension. God doesn't need us to be successful; God simply wants us to live our calling lovingly and to respond to his invitations. Like any of the difficulties that dot our lives, failure can be an opportunity to change our vantage point from our human perspective to one of faith. In faith, we can accept how God is working in our lives even when we can't see God's hand.

When we are successful, we often attribute our success to our own hard work. When we fail, we are often forced to admit that the results of our efforts are out of our hands. This is where failure (whether real or apparent) may be God's secret invitation to acknowledge that it is the Lord who blesses the results of what we do. God may even be inviting us to go further: to make a profound act of surrender by fully entrusting to God the results of all of our efforts. This is the profound act of surrender that enabled Saint Nöel Chabanel to offer his life to God.

Through the Day

Lord, I entrust myself to you completely.

———◆———

42 I live in the truth of who Jesus calls me to be in the world.

"It's all my fault!"

My stomach sank as I realized no one was coming. After all that work!

I went over to my co-worker, who had also sacrificed valuable time to prepare the event. When I apologized, she exploded with frustration.

"I'm banning the word 'sorry.' I'm tired of hearing it!"

I blanched. "What? I'm s—." I caught myself just in time.

"You're always saying that you're sorry for things that aren't your fault, as if you can control other people or the weather. But you're just not that powerful!" Having declared the ban, she relaxed into a smile.

Relieved, I tried to smile back, but her challenge had startled me. She was right. Often when things went wrong, my first reaction was to blame myself, even if it wasn't my fault. Maybe blaming myself was less scary than acknowledging that something was outside my control. I could see how falsely blaming myself could lead to an equally false sense of control: *if only I were better at . . . , everything would be fine.*

My friend had realized what took me a much longer time to see: that falsely blaming myself poisons my spirit—I fail to respect myself and the truth about who I am in the world.

From God's Heart to Yours

"[Y]ou will know the truth, and the truth will make you free" (Jn 8:32).

Hidden in the Darkness

Jesus came to bring the truth that God created us in love and for love: God loves us as we are. We do not need to feel trapped by guilt for everything bad that happens. Healthy guilt over our own sinfulness is a grace that can motivate us to learn, to change, and to grow from our mistakes. But false guilt for what we have no power over simply deflects our attention from what's really important.

When we blame ourselves for something that is not our fault, it is usually because we desperately want to feel a sense of control. Instead, we are living a lie: we deny the truth about ourselves and our real power to make choices. We become trapped in self-hate and shame, unable to live in the joy God intended for us.

Needing to feel a sense of control in our lives is a genuine human need. But trying to control something over which we have no power is simply a lie that distracts us from our true responsibilities.

When we concentrate on what we *are* responsible for, and let go of the things for which we aren't responsible, we experience a healthy sense of our own identity and power. God calls us to a unique way of being in the world and empowers us to fulfill our particular mission. Living the way God intended for us brings deep fulfillment, freedom, and joy. But we can only live our God-given calling when we have a strong, authentic sense of our true power—with all its gifts and limitations.

Jesus encourages us to live in the truth, to be secure in him. When we trust that God absolutely accepts us as we are, we will be free to find our way of being and living in the world. Secure in God's love and call, we can lovingly reach out to others and fulfill our mission in the world.

Through the Day

Jesus, empower me to live in the freedom of the truth of who I truly am.

———◀◉▶———

43 I seek to fulfill my God-given potential.

"What's the use of trying?"

Helen is a remarkably talented artist who has created some beautiful and daring pieces of art. Some years ago, after creating a particularly provocative and much admired piece, Helen stopped doing her art altogether. At first, her resistance was subtle: she said she'd do something "soon," but never got around to it. The "soon" turned to "someday," and next she started blaming the circumstances of her life, making them an excuse for not creating any more art.

Family and friends have tried to encourage her. Recently, one friend offered her several small venues to display and possibly sell her art when she is ready. Instead of jumping eagerly at the opportunity, Helen missed all the deadlines. Perhaps Helen is afraid she can't live up to the standards of her previous art. Or maybe it's easier for her to make excuses than to take another risk. It could even be that Helen is afraid of success.

From God's Heart to Yours

"For surely I know the plans I have for you, says the LORD, plans for your welfare and not for harm, to give you a future with hope" (Jer 29:11).

Hidden in the Darkness

God's love for us is not some generically positive mood-cloud hovering over the world. God's love for us is concrete and specific. God is "for you"; God is "for me." God has a concrete plan for each of us and deeply desires our well-being and a hope-filled future.

Yet, like Helen, some of us are afraid to act on our own behalf. We give up on ourselves. Our fears develop into the conviction that we are beyond hope, that we are unworthy of happiness, and so a positive future becomes inconceivable. If we have a bit of success, or the opportunity to follow a dream falls into our laps, we may even sabotage ourselves by creating a crisis or by failing at something easy (like missing a deadline). We may not be fully aware of how we are doing it, but our conviction that we are unworthy of success is so strong that we actually make success impossible.

But we *are* worthy of respect and of success. That God created us and loves us *makes us worthy human persons*. Our shame may trick us into thinking we are unworthy, but we need to let this false conviction die.

We can start by consciously bringing to mind the constant efforts God lovingly makes on our behalf, starting with the daily gifts: awaking each morning, the sunrise, coffee ... Each of these is a new opportunity God offers us. God renews our life every morning, presenting each new day to us as a gift. An essential part of our relationship with our Creator is to accept the gift of our life and to rejoice in it!

When we begin to accept that we are worthy of God's gift of life, we can also begin to live more fully: to act on our own behalf, to seek the joy and meaning of fulfilling our potential. We no longer need to be fearful of the future, because we know it is part of God's plan. No matter the difficulties the future may contain, we can trust that God will be there with us.

Through the Day

God of goodness, I gratefully offer back to you today one gift that I want to develop.

———◆———

44 I accept responsibility for my choices, not those of others.

"How am I not good enough?"

Bonnie, a beautiful and hard-working young mother, has just separated from her husband. Her world fell apart when she found out her husband was having an affair. Every day she blames herself in different, contradictory ways. Yesterday, she was convinced she was working too hard to provide for the family's future—she should have stayed at home more. Today she is sure she should have worked harder at her career and earned more money.

Bonnie needs to be honest about her part in their relationship, really looking at the ways she contributed to misunderstandings or created distance between her husband and herself. But the truth is, whatever choices Bonnie made, her husband made his own choices as well.

Unfortunately, Bonnie is convinced that his betrayal is completely her fault, that her husband wouldn't have been unfaithful to her if she were a better person. "What's wrong with me?" she muses darkly as she studies herself in the mirror, coaches her daughter on her first bike ride, or chairs a business meeting.

When we feel betrayed, it's often easier to blame ourselves than experience the full pain of betrayal. Self-blame becomes a coping mechanism that dulls our pain for the moment, and, in dire circumstances, can even allow us to survive the traumatic betrayal of abuse. And yet to live fully, we gradually need to let go of blaming ourselves for the choices that others make. Another's choices do not determine who we are becoming. Ours do.

From God's Heart to Yours

"You shall love your neighbor as yourself" (Mt 22:39).

Hidden in the Darkness

The Second Commandment contains a striking phrase that many of us overlook, perhaps because loving others can be so difficult. Yet these two neglected words—"as yourself"—can be the key to understanding this com-

mandment. Jesus says that in order to love others, we have
to know how to truly love ourselves.

True love of self has nothing to do with being selfish.
Loving ourselves begins with respecting ourselves: our
dignity as children of God, our individuality, our ability to
think, our free will to choose, and our vocation to love.

Likewise, while loving one another includes many
other elements—such as support, compassion, understanding, and self-sacrifice—the strength of any relationship between two people is founded on their respect for
each other. Freedom and individuality are God-given gifts
that are not to be taken lightly.

Both parties are responsible for growing in this love
and respect. Because we all have weaknesses, it can be
difficult at times to balance our own needs with how we
can lovingly respond to the other's needs. We make mistakes and choose poorly. The more we love each other, the
more hurt our bad choices cause.

Betrayal is one of the most painful choices of all; but if
we can take responsibility for our part—and only our
part—then, despite the tremendous pain, even betrayal
can become an opportunity to grow.

When we focus on our own choices, we live in the
truth that empowers us and sets us free—free to live our
life more fully, free to see a new beginning in the wide
range of choices before us, free to grow as God invites us,
even free to forgive when we are ready to receive this
grace.

Through the Day

Lord, thank you for the power and freedom to make my own choices.

———◄○►———

45 Forgiveness empowers and frees me.

"It's unforgivable!"

There are some things that just seem too big to forgive.

My dad was crossing the street on the way home from the bank when an elderly woman accelerated her car, hitting him. My dad died about 22 hours later of massive injuries, without ever regaining consciousness.

We all knew it was an accident; the elderly woman hadn't seen my dad and was horrified. A police officer who visited my mom told her how devastated the woman was. She was convinced that my entire family hated her.

As we were making funeral arrangements, my mother told us what the police officer had said. Despite her tremendous grief, Mom told us she was going to visit the woman that afternoon.

With one of my sisters, my mom drove to the woman's house and expressed her understanding and forgiveness. The elderly woman was greatly relieved and comforted by my mother's visit. When the police officer found out what my mom had done, he was amazed.

Even though I wasn't ready at that moment to make that visit with her, my mother's heroic act of forgiveness became a source of strength and comfort to all of us.

From God's Heart to Yours

"[B]e kind to one another, tenderhearted, forgiving one another, as God in Christ has forgiven you" (Eph 4:32).

Hidden in the Darkness

The Letter to the Ephesians reminds us that, as God is always ready to forgive us, so we are called to offer forgiveness to others. Though the pain of loss or betrayal can darken the landscape of our lives for years, when we are ready, forgiveness has the power to bring a new dawn.

To be a source of grace and healing, forgiveness must be real. Forgiveness is not pretending that we weren't hurt or that the offense was no big deal. It is not going back to the same place we were before. And, in cases of abuse in long-term relationships, forgiveness certainly does not mean putting ourselves in the situation of being abused again.

Forgiveness cannot be forced. If we pretend to forgive before we are ready, we can actually sabotage our own healing and our ability to forgive later on. Genuine forgiveness is an act of honesty about what happened, respect for the dignity of all the persons involved, and acceptance of our human condition. Forgiveness sometimes happens piece by piece, a gradual letting go that begins with a simple desire to be healed.

The journey to forgiveness is graced and mysterious. The ability to forgive goes beyond the ordinary power of the human heart. If we are struggling to forgive, we can tap into the power of the Our Father. As we experience God's mercy in our lives, we can pray for the grace to discern the difference between honestly acknowledging our feelings and fostering unhealthy resentment. We learn to forgive by knowing ourselves to be forgiven.

When we are ready to forgive, we stop clinging to our own deep pain. This selfless act creates a space for God to enter and pour out such abundant love and grace that they stream through us to others. Forgiveness doesn't stop our pain. But it frees us from the shadows of the past and empowers us to move into the future without shame, open to new life. When we forgive, we empower others to receive that same peace and freedom.

Through the Day

Lord, pour out on me your merciful love and the grace of a forgiving heart.

———◄o►———

46 I count on God's faithfulness in my sufferings.

"Where is God when I'm suffering?"

The story that will introduce today's meditation will be yours.

Pick a painful experience from your own life—something that was really hard, but for which the raw pain has passed, either because it happened a while ago or because you have come to terms with it. It could be the painful ending of a relationship, any kind of loss, the death of a loved one, or perhaps an accident.

Take some time to remember your experience, especially focusing on what strengthened you while you were going through it. How did you cope with it, even survive it? What choices did you have, and what choices did you make?

If the memories become too painful, bring your thoughts back to the present. That painful event has shaped you; it changed you; but it did not destroy you. You are here, and you are probably stronger because of it. How?

How has the passage of time or your efforts to cope with this event changed or deepened your understanding of what happened? Has what you've gone through given you strength, compassion, or skills for other situations in your life? How has going through this experience made you who you are today?

From God's Heart to Yours

"I want to know Christ and the power of his resurrection and the sharing of his sufferings by becoming like him in his death, if somehow I may attain the resurrection from the dead" (Phil 3:10–11).

Hidden in the Darkness

Pain and suffering are an inevitable part of human life, but the sufferings of our lives and the tragedies we experience or witness often uncover profound questions: Does God really love us? How can God allow this kind of suffering?

Theology can offer perspectives, but no answer can truly satisfy the pain behind these questions. In his Letter to the Philippians, Saint Paul doesn't attempt to give a theology of suffering but instead shares his own experience with us.

Since his conversion, Paul has centered his life on Christ. He has discovered that the amazing power of God that raised Jesus from the dead—transforming Jesus' death into resurrection—is at work in Paul's own life. Paul no longer needs to fear suffering and death because he knows that from them, God will bring life.

Only the awesome power of God could bring good out of the malevolence of sin. Out of the vindictive execution of his Son, God brings Christ's resurrection and the salvation of humanity. God's amazing love continually "makes the best" of human sinfulness. And because God dearly loves us, God is constantly making the best of our lives. Even when we suffer, even when we sin, God uses that pain or sinful choice to help us to grow, to draw nearer to Christ.

Paul's tremendous sufferings as an apostle—which he identified with Christ's sufferings on the cross—were touched and transformed by the power of Christ's resurrection. Looking back at the experience of suffering with which you began this meditation, can you see how God entered into your pain, guided you in it, and has used it to bring you to a new place in your life?

Our life in Christ doesn't take away the suffering that is part of human existence, but it transforms it. Because of Jesus, we can trust that God is always faithfully at work in our lives.

Through the Day

Crucified and risen Lord, I believe that you can bring life out of what I am suffering today.

————◦————

47 When doubts overwhelm me, I seek refuge in Jesus.

"I feel like God has abandoned me."

These are not the words we'd ascribe to Saint Therese of Lisieux. Many people imagine Saint Therese as a pious little girl who grew into a perfect nun. Raised by parents who are themselves candidates for canonization, joining the Carmelites at the age of fifteen, what wasn't perfect about her life? But if we examine the photographs, something in Therese's eyes reveals a glimpse of the real woman behind the legends.

We know from her writings that Therese didn't consider herself special. On the contrary, she saw herself as "little," even useless. Throughout her life she constantly strove to grasp the meaning of God's tremendous love. After Therese experienced the first symptoms of tuberculosis, she was enshrouded until her death in a spiritual darkness that tempted her to doubt the very existence of God. She talks about her soul being blindfolded and tormented by the darkness.

Therese had staked her entire life as a Carmelite sister on her relationship with God, the God whose very existence she was being tempted to doubt. But because she had nurtured her conviction that God loved her throughout her life, her faith-filled response to the shroud of doubt was to offer her sufferings for the salvation of others who doubted or rejected God.

Therese's way of total confidence in God's love was validated—not just by the official recognition of the Church, but by the many people who adopted her spirituality of confidence. Perhaps Therese, who took refuge in Jesus' love even when she couldn't feel his presence, can encourage us when our own doubts overwhelm us.

From God's Heart to Yours

"You are a hiding place for me; you preserve me from trouble; you surround me with glad cries of deliverance" (Ps 32:7).

Hidden in the Darkness

For many of us who are struggling to believe that we are lovable, doubt about God's love for us is a frequent visitor, if not a permanent guest. At these times when we feel desolate or overwhelmed, we need a "hiding place," a sanctuary to which we can retreat.

What would that ideal hiding place be like? A place where we are free to be ourselves, where we feel completely safe and can leave our struggles outside for the moment; a place where our weaknesses don't matter, where we are sure that we are loved without conditions, where no one else can invade, where we don't need to output so much as take in. The psalmist invites us to consider God as that hiding place.

The *Anima Christi* is a beautiful prayer that invites us to hide in Jesus' wounds. Jesus' wounded heart, pierced by the soldier's lance, is always open to us. Jesus' heart, broken for us, is the ultimate proof of God's love for us. When we feel trapped in a desert of doubt and parched in spirit, we need to let go of our doubts long enough to take refuge in his heart—even if we have to start by only pretending that Jesus loves us. If we ask Jesus to let us "hide" in him, then the doubts will eventually start to recede, or at least lose their power over us.

Like Saint Therese, we may be called to travel through the aridity of doubt for a great part of our lives. But our doubts don't need to rule us; instead, they can prompt us to seek the oasis of Jesus' heart.

Through the Day

Jesus, hide me in your heart.

———◁○▷———

48 God wants to give me the joy of following my dreams.

"If only I dared ..."

Bob was a well-paid engineer, but his dissatisfaction with his work—which he had never really liked—rapidly grew into frustration. His job required him to spend chunks of time away from his family, including a long daily commute into the city. Bob and his wife, Jenny, had decided to homeschool, and Bob wanted to be a big part of that. Jenny shared many of Bob's frustrations and struggled with her own.

They started dreaming together. Suppose they moved to a farm? A farm would be a healthy place for the children to grow up, they could both spend time with the children, and Bob could find ways to supplement their income.

By this time, Bob and Jenny had four children. Common sense (and friends) told them they were taking a huge risk. They made a backup plan, and, trusting in each other, followed their dream to create a new life for their family.

It wasn't easy—finding the right farm, dealing with tight finances, learning to raise livestock and grow crops.

Yet despite the struggles and setbacks, Bob and Jenny are both quick to admit that God guided them to follow their dream, and their family is happier because of it.

From God's Heart to Yours

"Take delight in the LORD, and he will give you the desires of your heart" (Ps 37:4).

Hidden in the Darkness

When we have trouble trusting ourselves, the kind of daring it takes to follow a dream can seem impossibly far away. Yet Psalm 37 reminds us that God, who knows our desires better than we do, *wants* to fulfill our dreams. Even if we can take only one baby step forward in trust, God blesses it abundantly.

Part of "delighting in God" is to trust that on the most basic level, God has made us competent for the situations of our life. God gives us not only the ability to cope, but also the gifts to participate in that divine work of giving new life. We are each called in some way to give life.

Our dreams can be a huge source of energy and life. Deep desires are often connected with our gifts; sometimes we discover our gifts only after we have begun to follow a particular dream or inspiration. When a dream is unacknowledged, the gift too often goes unrecognized. We risk losing a part of ourselves, or living with a smaller sense of ourselves. All of our dreams—even the most unrealistic—contain a seed of truth about our identity. Before we can discern whether a dream is an invitation from God or simply reflects an unfulfilled desire, we have to acknowledge it. Getting in touch with our dreams, even the impossible ones, revitalizes and energizes us.

The tremendous joy and energy associated with our dreams is what helps us overcome the seemingly impossible obstacles we must confront to make our dreams a reality. The energy we tap into that enables us to pursue our dreams can become a source of energy for our whole lives. The more we recognize how precious we are to God and how great God's desires are for us, the more we dare to entrust ourselves completely to God. Our dreams merge with God's dreams for us. This attitude of trust allows us to live in God's own peace and delight.

Through the Day

Life-giving Spirit, I dare to live in your loving dream for me.

———◆———

49 I choose to be guided by the light of God's love.

"Turn on the light!"

Belinda wakes from her nightmare gasping for breath. She frantically reaches for the lamp and turns it on. As her breathing slows, she sits up, hugging her pillow to her chest. Will she ever get used to the nightmares?

For years as a child, Belinda was sexually abused, first by her father and then her older brother. When Belinda turned twelve, her parents divorced and Belinda went to live with her mother. She tried to forget what happened, and she thought she had.

Five months ago the nightmares started to haunt her. Finally, Belinda's best friend asks her what is going on— her grades are plummeting; she walks around campus half-dead; she's lost interest in everything. Her friend is worried that Belinda is on drugs.

Although afraid to tell her friend, Belinda is more scared of being alone in her nightmares. She tells her friend a little about the past. She describes how she sits up all night, terrified of the darkness, until the night sky begins to brighten, when she'll finally drop off to sleep.

Her friend not only understands, but she also helps Belinda find someone to talk to. The counselor tells her that the darkness of terror, pain, and shame she is immersed in is typical for a survivor of sexual abuse, and that it might take a while, but that things will get better.

Belinda doesn't know it yet, but she is a strong woman who, with the support she is getting, will do more than survive. But it will be a long journey to the light, and to get there, she must choose to focus on the light.

From God's Heart to Yours

"It is you who light my lamp; the LORD, my God, lights up my darkness" (Ps 18:28).

Hidden in the Darkness

When we are immersed in the depths of a profound darkness like Belinda's, God feels absent. Yet, Psalm 18 assures us that God wants to be close to us all the time, to be our guiding light always, even involving himself in the gritty details of our lives.

Whether our lives are stormy or sunny right now, all of us need a beacon, a reference point to guide us to our desired destination. What or who we choose to guide us will make a radical difference in where and how we arrive. Belinda wants to arrive at a place free from fear, where she can once again have meaning and purpose in her life. Where do we want to go?

One of the sisters in my community has filled the walls of her office with images of lighthouses. The lighthouse reminds her to watch for the secret messages of unconditional love God "flashes" to her. God's love is the beacon guiding her life.

God wants to companion us, too, through our entire lives. God wants to *be* our light—that is what the promise of heaven is all about. "And there will be no more night; they need no light of lamp or sun, the Lord God will be their light" (Rev 22:5).

God will continue to shine the light of his love throughout our lives in a multitude of ways. The question is whether we will pay attention.

What manifestation of God's love will become the guiding light of our lives?

Through the Day

Lord, shine your love like a beacon in my day, and guide me to you.

———◄○►———

50 God works through both my successes and failures.

"My best just isn't good enough!"

In 1900, a young Italian seminarian, James Alberione, failed in following his call. He had felt called to be a priest since he was six years old. His family had sacrificed for him to attend seminary. But at sixteen, James was expelled, most likely for reading books that were considered unorthodox. Back home on the farm, James felt lost. He had no idea what to do. Finally his mother encouraged him to speak with their parish priest. Realizing James had simply been misled, the priest helped him enter another seminary. He would be on probation, but at least his dream still had a chance.

Four months later during his Eucharistic adoration, praying over the needs of the Church and still on probation, James received Jesus' invitation to his life's work—to proclaim the Good News through the means of communication. His vision inspired others to join him. Today thousands live the Pauline spirituality that Blessed James Alberione shared with the world.

James could have just given up or tried to get back into his old seminary. But at the new seminary, James found the guidance and inspiration he needed to fulfill God's call—guidance that he might never have received if he hadn't been expelled. God chose to work through James' failure to lead him in a new direction.

From God's Heart to Yours

"[R]ekindle the gift of God that is within you through the laying on of my hands; for God did not give us a spirit of cowardice, but rather a spirit of power and of love and of self-discipline" (2 Tim 1:6).

Hidden in the Darkness

This passage advises Timothy and us not to become discouraged when things get rough, but to stir up God's gift of the Spirit, who enlivens the gifts we have received to live our calling. Yet, this is difficult advice to live when we are confronted with failure.

Anytime we try something new or follow a dream, we risk failure. If we never try anything new, we'll never develop new abilities or find out what we are truly capable of doing. The challenges we confront can push us to excel and reach further. But sometimes the challenges are too much for us, or our limits prevent us from succeeding in the way we'd hoped.

Admitting failure is never easy, but it doesn't have to be devastating. Failure can help us honestly assess and accept our unique combination of gifts, strengths, and limitations. Failure can also help point us in a new direction that we would never have chosen on our own. Facing failure can even help us grow in humility—reminding us of the truth that our value does not lie in what we accomplish, but in how much God loves us.

In God's eyes, our "failure" may not be a failure at all. Perhaps what we learned is invaluable. Maybe a project didn't achieve the desired results, but helped form a wonderful collaborative team for a future project. We will never fully understand God's mysterious plan for us, but we can trust that God can take anything life throws at us and work in it for our good and for the good of the world.

Failure might even be an invitation to grow in fidelity—to be able to persevere in our efforts without any tangible indication of success. This kind of deep faith would delight God and allow the Spirit to work freely in us.

Through the Day

Lord, I entrust my efforts to you; do with me whatever you will.

———◀◉▶———

51 I trust that God gives me the grace for the challenges I face.

"I can't do it!"

As I got close to finishing this book, self-doubt set in. "Have I been deceiving myself?" I thought. "Have all my efforts been useless?" When I was making my hour of adoration later that day, I brought my doubts and fears before Jesus and asked whether he was speaking to me through my misgivings.

In Jesus' presence, I tried to stop thinking about what I wanted, or what others might think of me. I offered him the book, my efforts, and my fears—all were his. And then I sat before him, tears in my eyes, waiting for him to respond. My waiting, listening heart became my prayer.

Then one of the sisters read aloud from the end of the Gospel of Matthew—the sending of the apostles. I let the words from the Gospel reverberate inside me. And I felt something stirring. *"Go! . . ."* Jesus' voice was not in the doubts and fears. Instead, Jesus was inviting me to go forward and finish the book. I could let go of the doubts and fears because he would fulfill his promise to do what he planned with it.

When we are doing something difficult, all of us wonder at some point if we can actually pull it off. Our own fears or self-doubts can cripple us or prevent us from doing something just because it's new or hard.

From God's Heart to Yours

"Go. . . . And remember, I am with you always, to the end of the age" (Mt 28:19–20).

Hidden in the Darkness

God's words, "I am with you," are repeated throughout the Bible, especially toward those who feel afraid or unworthy: from Moses (Ex 3:11–12) to Jeremiah (Jer 1:6–8), to the apostles before they received the Spirit. When we feel incapable of carrying out whatever is before us, those divine words are meant to reassure us, too. Jesus promises to be with his disciples—both then and now—specifically in the power and grace of the Spirit.

The Spirit can make up for anything we lack or fear. We might feel overawed by the responsibility of raising a child or of making decisions that will impact others' lives. Our fears might blind us to everything except the ways we could fail, making us feel inadequate. But if we spend too much time fretting, we could miss the grace of the Spirit.

When we allow the clamor of doubt and anxiety to take over, we cannot hear the voice of the Spirit within us, inviting us to live our calling with joy, peace, and fruitfulness. At these times, we need to free our sight from fear's narrow tunnel vision.

When I need to enlarge my perspective, I often turn to Beethoven's symphonies. Beethoven is one of the most amazing composers of all time; his beautiful music is so elegantly simple that it is easily accessible, yet so advanced that musicians and theorists are *still* trying to figure him out. In one of my favorite pieces—his Fifth Symphony— Beethoven's genius takes just two little notes in one simple pattern—*duh-duh-duh-da*—and makes them the theme of one of the most famous pieces of music.

If two little notes in the hands of Beethoven could become the great Fifth Symphony, what can we become, in the hands of our loving God?

Through the Day

Come, Holy Spirit, and fill me with your grace and power.

———◁◦▷———

52 I accept Jesus' invitation to live in him.

"What's the right way to go?"

I am directionally challenged. I can get lost in a parking lot, or going around the block. I used to feel terribly ashamed about it, but now I just prepare well before I drive anywhere new. I look up my own directions, ask advice about routes with the least traffic, mark my map, and leave extra time in case I get lost. The key for me is to use the map to visualize the way ahead of time, keeping it handy so that if one way is blocked, I can easily find alternatives.

The personal journeys we make to grow in faith and healthy self-esteem have many more obstacles than any physical journey. But in our spiritual journey, there is a secure Way that we can follow.

From God's Heart to Yours

"I am the way, and the truth, and the life. No one comes to the Father except through me" (Jn 14:6).

Hidden in the Darkness

At the Last Supper, Jesus chose to describe himself as *the* Way, Truth, and Life. This threefold description Jesus gives of himself can help us to understand better how he communicates with us and how he invites us to grow in our relationships.

Jesus as our Way surely invites us to imitate the way of love that he lived—to love God, ourselves, and others as he does. But Jesus wants to be much more than our model because he says, "I *am* the Way," not "I show you the way." It's as if Jesus is saying he is the perfect map; the smoothest, most direct road; the most satisfying rest stops; and the best driving companion—all in one. When we invite Jesus into our lives, whether we feel it or not, we will never be alone, because Jesus *is* our journey. In everything we experience in our lives, every choice we make, Jesus is lovingly present.

Likewise, Jesus *is* our Truth in his very person. Jesus doesn't just reveal the truth of God's unconditional love for us but is the perfect expression of God's faithful love for us. Jesus *is* God's "I love you" to humanity! As our Truth, Jesus brings our negative thoughts, our false assumptions, and our cynical attitudes into relationship with him and transforms them. Jesus invites us to believe in the truth not only about God but also about us: Jesus calls us "beloved."

Jesus as our Life is perhaps the most striking metaphor of all. People who are deeply in love sometimes call their beloved their "life." Jesus is that Beloved One, both for us and for the Father. Jesus died and rose for us so that our lives could be transformed into his, so that we could share fully in his divine life of love. When Jesus' life becomes our own, we are adopted into the most perfect family ever, sharing in Jesus' intimate communion with the Father and Spirit! We are immersed in the love-life of the Trinity, our hearts embraced by Love.

As our Way, Truth, and Life, Jesus invites us not only to follow his way of truth that brings life, but to unite our entire being with him—our choices and actions with his way, our thoughts and attitudes with his truth, our sentiments and desires with his life. United to Christ and secure in his love, we then become the loving face of Christ for others.

Through the Day

Jesus, be my Way, my Truth, and my Life!

———◄◦►———

A New Beginning

Low self-esteem easily traps us in a downward spiral. Becoming secure in God's love can be a very difficult journey out of that cycle. As we prayed with these meditations, perhaps we have come to a new awareness of our own self-worth and of how much God loves us. It might prove helpful later on if we take time now to describe this deeper understanding of ourselves and our relationship with God, even writing it down. Later, we may appreciate being able to revisit the fruit of this journey, perhaps at a point when our new awareness is challenged.

I hope that during this time we have also developed a new pattern with these meditations—perhaps a new way to pray daily, or the habit of challenging our negative assumptions, or the custom of rooting our deeper times of prayer in Scripture. Whatever new pattern of thought or prayer we have developed, we can focus on bringing it into the next stage of our journey. God's gentle and powerful love will build on our personal efforts, and eventually break the cycle of low self-esteem and transform our fears into a greater trust—in God and in ourselves.

As a Daughter of Saint Paul, I pray for everyone I encounter—whether in person or through what I've written. I will continue to pray for you on your journey toward spiritual wholeness, that you may come to live in the truth of God's love for you, the joy of following Christ more closely, and the loving embrace of the Spirit.

Suggestions for Praying with Sacred Scripture

For many, the Bible is an untapped treasure that we feel we are not wise or prayerful enough to understand. We may even feel intimidated, thinking we need a secret key to unlock the Bible. Hopefully, praying with the meditations in this book has shown us that the secret key is God's *desire* to communicate with us. And we want to respond to his desire and listen more deeply to his Word.

Because the Bible is God's Word spoken to us, we need only open our hearts and learn how to listen. Not a passive "just being there," but a listening that is thirsty, that hangs on every syllable; a listening as eager as that of new lovers who anticipate the first whispered affirmations of their beloved.

The meditations in this book are a good start in learning how to meditate on our own. Below, I've outlined concrete steps for those who are just beginning to meditate on the Word of God. At the end of this appendix, I've list-

ed several other methods for praying with the Word of
God, along with resources to get started.

How to Begin Meditating
on the Word of God

Here are some simple steps we can use as we begin
making meditation on our own. After describing each step,
I've included an example from my personal meditation.

1.   We choose a passage.

Before we begin, we choose a passage of Scripture for
prayer. If we are just beginning, it helps to start with the
Gospels. We could slowly work our our way through a
particular book of the Bible, pray with readings from the
Mass of the day, or choose a passage that seems to suit our
needs that day, perhaps from this book.

*I have chosen to use the Scripture passage from the first med-
itation in this book: "[Y]ou are precious in my sight, and honored, and I love you" (Isa 43:4).*

2.   We invite the Holy Spirit to enlighten us.

Our invitation can be in our own words or in the form
of a familiar prayer. This invitation to the Spirit can also
become our cue to slow down, take several deep breaths,
and become more receptive. One of my personal favorites
is the hymn *Veni Creator Spiritus*. The poetic rhythm—
whether in English or in Latin—calls me to attentiveness.

3. We read the chosen passage slowly and
    attentively.

If possible, we may read the Scripture aloud. It is most
important to pay close attention to the text, even reading
the passage through slowly two or three times. What do we
notice about the passage? Perhaps we notice a particular
word or a detail in the story, or something that puzzles us.

If the Scripture passage is a scene from the Gospel, we
might take a few minutes after we have read it to imagine
ourselves present at the scene. What does Jesus say?
Whom do we identify with in the story? What do we feel
as Jesus interacts with those around him? Does Jesus speak
to us?

*This passage from Isaiah uses direct address—it's God
speaking directly to me. I am a bit overwhelmed by the emotion
in these words—God is telling me directly that he loves me. I
notice two words—"precious" and "honored." What does it
mean to say that God "honors" me?*

4. We reflect on how God's Word is speaking to
    us here and now.

We apply what God is saying to us in our own lives, in
our current situation. Sometimes God's Word might comfort us; at other times it might challenge us or help us to
see our situation in a new way.

*I realize that, at first, I am feeling a bit uncomfortable with
the extravagance of these words. How could God find me precious? But I remind myself that God is speaking through this
passage to me, today. Maybe it would help if I could hear God's*

tone as he says these words. Maybe then they wouldn't seem so unbelievable. I close my eyes and imagine the Father whispering these words to me. Something in my heart thrills. Could God love me that much? I open my eyes. I remember other passages from the Gospels in which Jesus talks about how much God loves us, as when Jesus said, "As the Father has loved me, so I have loved you; abide in my love" (Jn. 15:9). I repeat the words that have touched my heart that they might sink in more deeply: "You are precious in my sight."

5. We ponder God's invitation and pray for the grace to live as God has invited us to live.

Now that God's Word has touched us, we reflect on how God might be inviting us to respond and to grow in love, and we pray for the grace to live that invitation.

I wonder if God is inviting me to trust in his love for me. I decide to carry these words with me today, and to allow the joy that I feel in being precious to God to shine through by smiling and being more patient with others. I pray for the grace to be able to take in and remember how much God loves me.

6. We conclude with a prayer of gratitude— usually the Our Father.

In our concluding prayer, we offer God our gratitude for the gift of his communication with us, and we pray to live the grace God has given us in the meditation.

Our Father . . .

RESOURCE:

Rosage, David. *Speak, Lord, Your Servant Is Listening: A Daily Guide to Scriptural Prayer*. Cincinnati: Servant Books, 2003. A helpful guide for those just beginning to meditate daily, with a list of Scripture readings for every day of the year.

Other Ways of Praying with Sacred Scripture

Below are several other methods and resources that can help us to pray more deeply with the Word of God.

Kodell, Jerome. *The Catholic Bible Study Handbook: A Popular Introduction to Studying Scripture*, Second Revised Edition. Cincinnati: Servant Books, 2001. An excellent introduction to reading, studying, and praying with Scripture. The section on prayer introduces several ways of approaching Scripture.

Liturgy of the Hours

The Liturgy of the Hours, also known as *Christian Prayer*, is the Church's official prayer. Made up primarily of the psalms, canticles, and readings from the Bible, *The Liturgy of the Hours* is a rich way of praying that has been used for centuries.

At the heart of *The Liturgy of the Hours* is the Book of Psalms, which Jesus himself must have prayed frequently. The psalms are an honest and intimate way of addressing

God; they are also poetry and always include sentiments of praise, encouraging us to turn our focus away from ourselves and toward God. Praying *The Liturgy of the Hours* weaves these attitudes of relating to God—honesty, praise, and intimacy—into the rhythm of our day.

RESOURCES:

Christian Prayer: The Liturgy of the Hours. Boston: Daughters of St. Paul, 1976. The prayer of the Church in one volume.

Shorter Christian Prayer. New York: Catholic Book Publishing, 1988. This shorter version includes just the two most frequently prayed hours of morning and evening prayer.

www.universalis.com. Universalis Publishing of London. This helpful Web site includes descriptions of the hours of prayer, how to pray them, and the prayers for the day.

Contemplating Scripture

Scripture passages can also be a springboard to a deeper prayer of silence. This simple prayer can take less than five minutes or continue for longer than a half hour. We use a short Scripture passage as a mantra to focus our attention on God and rest in God's heart.

RESOURCES:

Hermes, Kathryn James. *The Journey Within: Prayer as a Path to God*. Cincinnati: Servant Books, 2004. An excellent guide for deeper prayer. Chapter 16 introduces several ways of praying with Scripture.

Lectio Divina

Another wonderful way of praying with the Scriptures is *lectio divina*. Introduced widely by the Benedictines, *lectio divina* is so popular that there are many methods that concretize this simple yet profound way of praying.

RESOURCES:

Hall, Thelma. *Too Deep for Words: Rediscovering Lectio Divina with 500 Scripture Texts for Prayer*. Mahwah, NJ: Paulist Press, 1988.

Bosetti, Elena. *Mark: The Risk of Believing*. Boston: Pauline Books & Media, 2006. An excellent resource for praying with the Gospel of Mark.

APPENDIX B

Additional Resources

On the Examen of Consciousness:

Aschenbrenner, George. *The Examination of Conscience*. Chicago: Loyola Press, 2007. A short booklet that succinctly introduces the examen of consciousness.

Gallagher, Timothy M. *The Examen Prayer*. New York: Crossroad Publishing Company, 2006. An in-depth look at the core principles of the examen prayer and how it transforms our spiritual lives.

On the Little Way of Saint Therese of Lisieux:

D'Elbee, Jean C. J. *I Believe in Love: A Personal Retreat Based on the Teaching of St. Therese of Lisieux*. Translated by Marilyn Teichert, with Madeleine Stebbins. Manchester, NH: Sophia Institute Press, 2001. An in-depth and persuasive presentation of Saint Therese's spirituality.

Therese de Lisieux. *The Story of a Soul: the Autobiography of St. Therese of Lisieux*, Third Edition, translated by John Clarke. Washington, D.C.: ICS Publications, 1996. Saint Therese in her own words.

On Self-Esteem:

Branden, Nathaniel. *The Six Pillars of Self-Esteem*. New York: Bantam, 1994. One of the most insightful secular self-help books on self-esteem. (Please note, however, that the author makes a few references to some teachings of Christianity that do not reflect our faith-perspective as Catholics.)

Burns, David D. *Ten Days to Self-Esteem*. New York: Quill, 1993. A mainstream self-help workbook that gives practical strategies to assess, evaluate, and replace the inaccurate, negative thoughts that can often trigger feelings of worthlessness.

Froehle, Virginia Ann. *Loving Yourself More: 101 Meditations on Self-Esteem for Women*. Notre Dame, IN: Ave Maria Press, 2007. A good resource to continue developing self-esteem in the light of God's love for us.

Topical Index

abandoned, 13, 20, 75, 82, 96, 98, 119, 137

abuse, 13, 129, 132, 142

acceptance, 21, 28, 40, 44, 45, 48, 59, 62, 68, 78, 90, 95, 104, 109, 115, 122, 125, 127, 133, 146, 150

accomplishment, 26, 51, 78, 105

action, 26, 41, 45, 52, 83, 92, 107, 152

anger, 30, 59, 83, 84

anxiety, 35, 68, 87, 94, 103, 149

appreciation, 65, 90

attitude, 10, 44, 48, 53, 74, 92, 100, 106, 141, 151, 152

beauty, 54, 99, 100

betrayal, 59, 129, 130, 132

blame, 21, 42, 106, 124, 125, 128, 129

    blaming God, 118

blessings, 48, 49, 59, 98, 114

boundaries, 114

brokenness, 98, 119, 120, 139

burdens, 49, 67, 68

challenges, 55, 119, 146, 147

change, 26, 30, 40, 42, 93, 101, 102, 103, 122

choices, 26, 41, 49, 52, 63, 74, 85, 93, 107, 109, 125, 128, 129, 130, 134, 152

comparisons, 73, 74
compassion, 44, 68, 85
competition, 73, 74
confession. *See* Reconciliation, Sacrament of
control, 26, 71, 80, 87, 103, 107, 124
criticism, 91, 92
cross, 97, 120, 136

dependence, 41, 94, 95
desires, 27, 60, 68, 90, 133, 141, 152
disappointment, 59, 61
discernment, 92, 95, 133
discouragement, 92, 146
doubts. *See* self-doubt
dreams, 139, 140, 146

efforts, 21, 26, 74, 120, 121, 123, 134, 147
emptiness. *See* loneliness
examen of consciousness, 41
expectations, 68, 71, 93, 105
experiences, 17, 28, 31, 77, 85, 90, 91, 134, 136, 151

failure, 16, 26, 54, 105, 121, 122, 145, 146, 147
faith, 39, 71, 119, 122, 147
fatigue, 67, 68
faults, 24, 40, 42, 44, 63
fear, 13, 35, 51, 61, 66, 69, 76, 86, 87, 113, 127, 147, 148
feelings, 9, 24, 31, 59, 75, 76, 77, 78, 83, 85, 88, 90, 115, 133
focus, 29, 39, 46, 48, 51, 52, 63, 82, 100, 109, 130
forgiveness, 45, 46, 63, 131, 132, 133
fragility, 117
freedom, 39, 52, 109, 125, 130, 133
friends, 37, 38, 64, 65, 66, 90
future, 42, 71, 127, 128, 133

gentleness, 44, 68, 104, 105, 106

gifts, 10, 24, 29, 39, 114, 117, 141

    giftedness, 29, 48, 74, 82, 115, 117

God's faithfulness, 11, 36, 95, 97, 100, 103, 120, 134

God's love, 11, 13, 15, 19, 21, 26, 35, 50, 51, 52, 53, 55, 63, 66, 68, 95, 100, 108, 115, 125, 127, 138, 142, 144, 151

    loving kindness, 75

    merciful love, 24

    unconditional love, 13, 14, 16, 19, 144, 151

God's plan, 26, 109, 128

God's providence, 19, 32, 88

goodness, 44, 59, 68

grace, 24, 41, 46, 48, 71, 74, 78, 82, 101, 117, 124, 130, 132, 133, 147

gratitude, 29, 49, 73, 98

grief. *See* Loss

growth, 21, 29, 41, 55, 63, 80, 92, 102, 124, 130, 136, 146, 151

guide, 136, 142, 143

guilt, 9, 24, 41, 45, 47, 64, 81, 82, 83, 123, 124

happiness, 27, 28, 127

harshness, 68, 106

healing, 55, 63, 120, 132

honesty, 32, 40, 62, 77, 133, 146

hope, 29, 44, 59, 60, 76

humility, 41, 42, 68, 117, 146

identity, 10, 26, 44, 52, 74, 113, 115, 117, 125, 141

illusions, 63, 71, 100

inadequacy, 9, 24, 68, 73, 149

integrity, 85, 113

invitation, 72, 88, 89, 91, 117, 122, 147, 150

joy, 28, 31, 49, 65, 125, 139, 149

lack, 39, 149

life, 28, 38, 47, 52, 61, 62, 65, 82, 101, 127, 136, 141, 152

limitations, 13, 69, 80, 108, 116, 125, 146

loneliness, 38, 61, 88, 89, 90, 113

loss, 28, 55, 96, 98, 132, 134

lovable, 45, 51, 138

mercy, 24, 47, 80, 82, 133

mission, 45, 125

mistakes, 14, 15, 16, 43, 46, 124, 130

needs, 19, 21, 26, 34, 44, 51, 60, 76, 82, 87, 88, 95, 98, 107, 113, 125, 130, 138

negativity, 54, 75, 83

past, 42, 133

peace, 27, 44, 76, 133, 141, 149

perfectionism, 69, 70, 107

perseverance, 147

perspective, 15, 46, 49, 53, 67, 70, 79, 85, 122, 149

potential, 10, 28, 39, 68, 105, 126, 128

power, 24, 52, 63, 105, 125, 130, 131, 133, 135, 139

prayer, 21, 29, 31, 32, 37, 49, 60, 76, 79, 133

promises, 16, 60, 69, 71, 103, 144, 149

prove myself, 50, 51, 67

Reconciliation, Sacrament of, 30, 42, 47

refreshment, 55, 65, 76

rejection, 12, 13, 39, 105, 113, 122

relationship with God, God, 21, 26, 30, 41, 47, 63, 75, 90, 98, 127, 137, 151

relationships, 12, 41, 46, 65, 90, 93, 105, 114, 130, 151

renewal, 47, 55, 82, 127

respect, 106, 114, 124, 127, 130, 133

responsibility, 42, 130

 responsibilities, 125

restore,61, 64, 77

results, 26, 69, 71, 122, 123

resurrection, 13, 120, 135

sacrifices, 32, 34, 130

safe. *See* security

security, 27, 50, 52, 71, 88, 103, 138

self-awareness, 41, 47, 49, 61, 76, 89, 127

self-blame. *See* blame

self-confidence, 9, 51

self-deception, 63

self-doubt, 9, 37, 60, 82, 137, 138, 139

self-esteem, 10, 21, 26, 28, 39, 44, 49, 52, 62, 63, 80, 114, 117, 150, 153

self-giving, 34, 37

self-hatred, 1, 2, 42, 44, 49, 76, 125

self-image, 10, 74

self-sufficient, 95

self-worth, 9, 22, 24, 26, 38, 39, 51, 63, 80, 127, 128, 149

service, 45, 73, 105

shame, 24, 45, 46, 47, 62, 86, 87, 92, 125

silence, 75, 76, 106

sinfulness, 47, 62, 80, 82, 135

success, 71, 122, 127, 145, 147

suffering, 28, 49, 118, 119, 134, 135

surrender, 35, 123

thoughts, 52, 75, 77, 91, 151, 152

trust, 11, 21, 25, 60, 70, 78, 109, 141

truth, 42, 63, 114, 125

unique, 24, 39, 44, 72, 74, 85, 109, 114, 117, 125, 146
unworthiness. *See* self-worth

vulnerability, 66, 79, 87, 108

weakness, 14, 79, 108, 117
worry, 35, 37, 68, 69
worthiness. *See* self-worth

As a Daughter of St. Paul, Sister Marie Paul Curley finds inspiration and joy in daily Eucharistic adoration and in the Pauline mission of communicating Christ through the media. A former video producer, Sister Marie Paul writes books and screenplays, and assists young women to discern the call of God in their lives. She has a B.A. in communication from Emmanuel College, Boston. Her previous books include Bread of Life: Prayers for Eucharistic Adoration.

Other books of interest from Pauline Books & Media

How to Handle Worry: A Catholic Approach

Marshall J. Cook

Today's world is busy and non-stop—one filled with eighty-hour-work weeks and too little time left over. Author Marshall Cook offers a practical approach to deal with the worries and anxieties that creep into our chaotic lives. He explains how we can create and maintain harmony in our lives through faith and prayer. Begin your own journey toward serenity today!

0-8198-3390-8 $12.95 U.S.

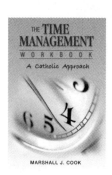

Time Management A Catholic Approach

By Marshall J. Cook

Combining the spiritual with the practical, Cook presents a resource for anyone feeling the crunch of time, the stress of day-to-day life. Filled with practical suggestions, inspiring examples, and reminders that we're all "on God's time," *Time Management: A Catholic Approach* will surely become a standout on your bookshelf.

0-8198-74299 $12.95 U.S.

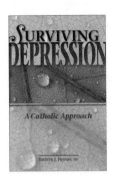

Surviving Depression: A Catholic Approach

Kathryn J. Hermes, FSP

Depression can strike anyone, even those deeply committed to living the Christian life. This reassuring book includes: encouraging stories of others who have lived with depression; psychological, medical, spiritual and practical self-care perspectives; tips for friends and family of the depressed.

0-8198-7077-3 $12.95 U.S.

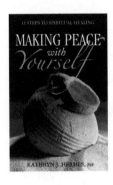

Making Peace with Yourself: 15 Steps to Spiritual Healing

Kathryn J. Hermes, FSP

"This is a guide to the deepest reality at work in our lives: God's presence in the midst of life's confusion. "This book explores the stories of people like you and me, people faced with situations that often were irreparable, people who need to make peace with themselves"

— *Kathryn J. Hermes, FSP*

0-8198-4859-X $12.95 U.S.

Order at www.pauline.org, or by calling
Pauline Books & Media at 1-800-876-4463,
or through the book and media center nearest you.

BOOKS & MEDIA

A mission of the Daughters of St. Paul

As apostles of Jesus Christ, evangelizing today's world:

We are CALLED to holiness
by God's living Word and Eucharist.

We COMMUNICATE the Gospel message
through our lives and through all
available forms of media.

We SERVE the Church
by responding to the hopes and needs
of all people with the Word of God,
in the spirit of St. Paul.

For more information visit our website:
www.pauline.org.

BOOKS & MEDIA

The Daughters of St. Paul operate book and media centers at the following addresses. Visit, call, or write the one nearest you today, or find us at www.paulinestore.org.

CALIFORNIA
  3908 Sepulveda Blvd, Culver City, CA 90230   310-397-8676
  3250 Middlefield Road, Menlo Park, CA 94025   650-369-4230
FLORIDA
  145 S.W. 107th Avenue, Miami, FL 33174   305-559-6715
HAWAII
  1143 Bishop Street, Honolulu, HI 96813   808-521-2731
ILLINOIS
  172 North Michigan Avenue, Chicago, IL 60601   312-346-4228
LOUISIANA
  4403 Veterans Memorial Blvd, Metairie, LA 70006   504-887-7631
MASSACHUSETTS
  885 Providence Hwy, Dedham, MA 02026   781-326-5385
MISSOURI
  9804 Watson Road, St. Louis, MO 63126   314-965-3512
NEW YORK
  115 E. 29th Street, New York City, NY 10016   212-754-1110
SOUTH CAROLINA
  243 King Street, Charleston, SC 29401   843-577-0175
TEXAS
  No book center; for parish exhibits or outreach evangelization, contact:
  210-569-0500, or SanAntonio@paulinemedia.com, or P.O. Box 761416,
  San Antonio, TX 78245
VIRGINIA
  1025 King Street, Alexandria, VA 22314   703-549-3806
CANADA
  3022 Dufferin Street, Toronto, ON M6B 3T5   416-781-9131